AF386326

GRAHAM DAY

MONOPRINTED PAINTINGS FOR

THE CONFERENCE OF THE BIRDS

EDITED BY ROSE ISSA

THE CONFERENCE OF THE BIRDS SERIES

The Conference, The Canticle or Parliament of the Birds (Manteq at-Tayr) was written by the Persian mystic Farid ud-Din Attar, a well-travelled poet, in 1177. He was born in Nishapur, and settled in his hometown where he kept a pharmacy (hence his name *Attar*, the perfume maker) while writing his poems. Later in his life he was tried for heresy and banished, while his property was looted.

Attar's best-known work is a *mathnavi*, i.e. a poem in rhyming couplets, an animal fable that involves the birds of the world searching for their spiritual king, the mythological Simurgh. The birds represent a range of human archetypes, such as the timid finch and the coy duck. They elect the hoopoe – because of its knowledge of the world gained while acting as courier between King Solomon and Bilqis, the queen of Sheba – to lead them to their ideal monarch. Each bird expresses its reservations and apprehensions about the journey ahead; each in turn is placated by the hoopoe.

The journey takes them over seven valleys (Quest, Knowledge, Bewilderment, Love, Detachment, Nothingness and Unity) that chart the progress of the aspirant. Only thirty birds survive the arduous voyage and these thirty (*si* in Farsi) birds (*murgh*) finally come face to face with the Simurgh. This pun is the crux of the tale: they are confronted by themselves.

Attar's work remains a testament to the possibility of the fulfilment, or, in a term used by mystics, the fruition of the human spirit – it is above all, as is Sufism as a whole, of an intensely humanistic nature.

Sources of Attar's story can be found in an earlier poem in the *Diwan* of Sana'i, in which the different cries of the birds are interpreted as the birds' way of calling on or praising God. A second source may have been the *Kalila wa Dimna*; this extraordinarily popular work, also called the *Fables of Bidpai*, originated in India and was translated into many languages. Another work which probably influenced Attar's allegory is the Arabic treatise *The Bird* by Avicenna. This is the first-person narrative of a bird (clearly representing the human soul) who is freed from a cage by other birds, and then flies off with his new companions on a journey to the 'Great King'.[1]

The imagery in Graham Day's monoprints is derived from popular talismans found in the Middle East and India. Zoomorphic calligraphy is not exclusively Persian, Arabic or Turkish. It has more to do with human curiosity and ingenuity than with a so-called prohibition on image-making, something that is only forbidden in religious places. The pious pictures are often associated with the Bektashi order, whose origins

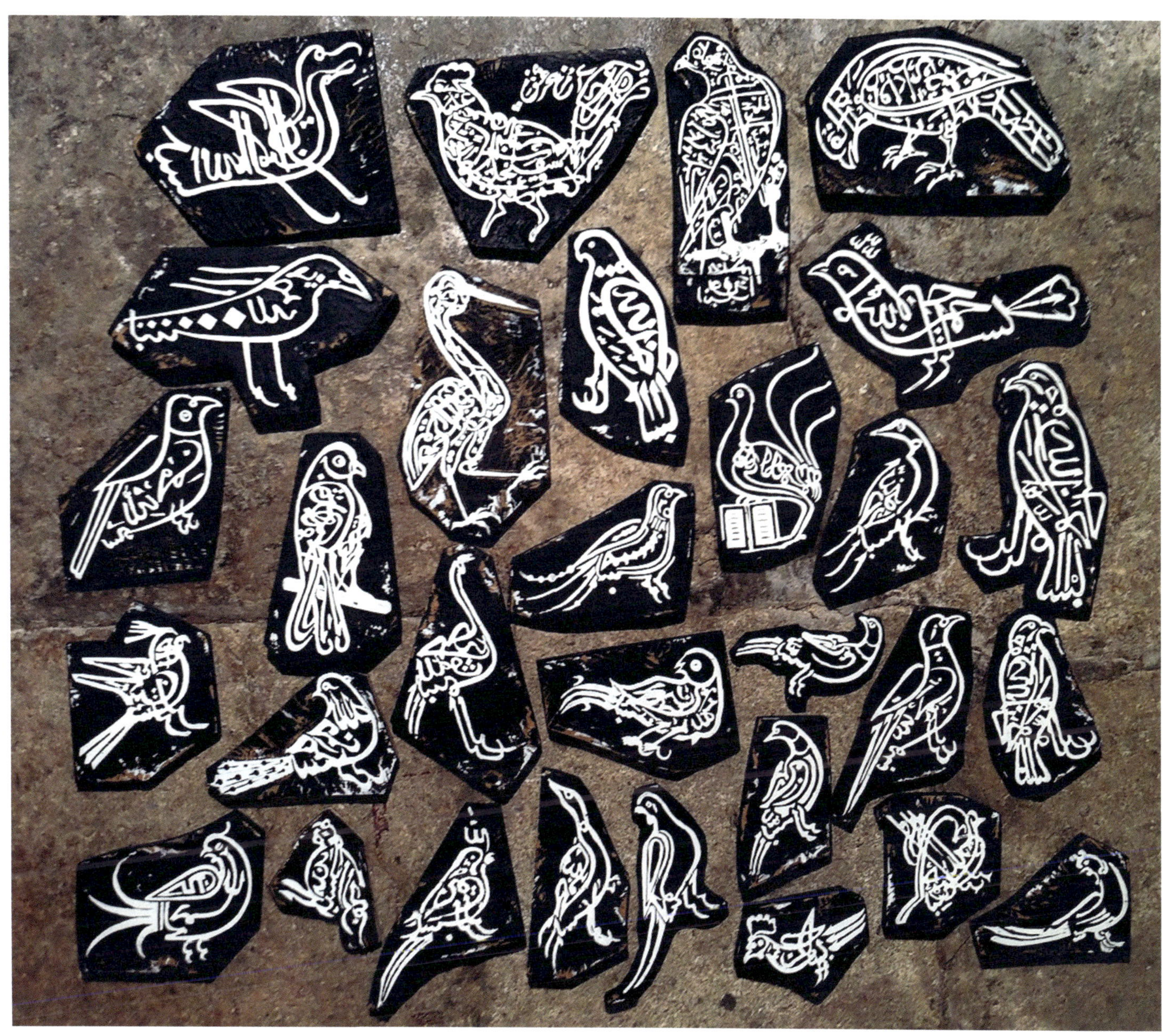

Thirty lino cuts, mounted on wood, carved by Graham Day

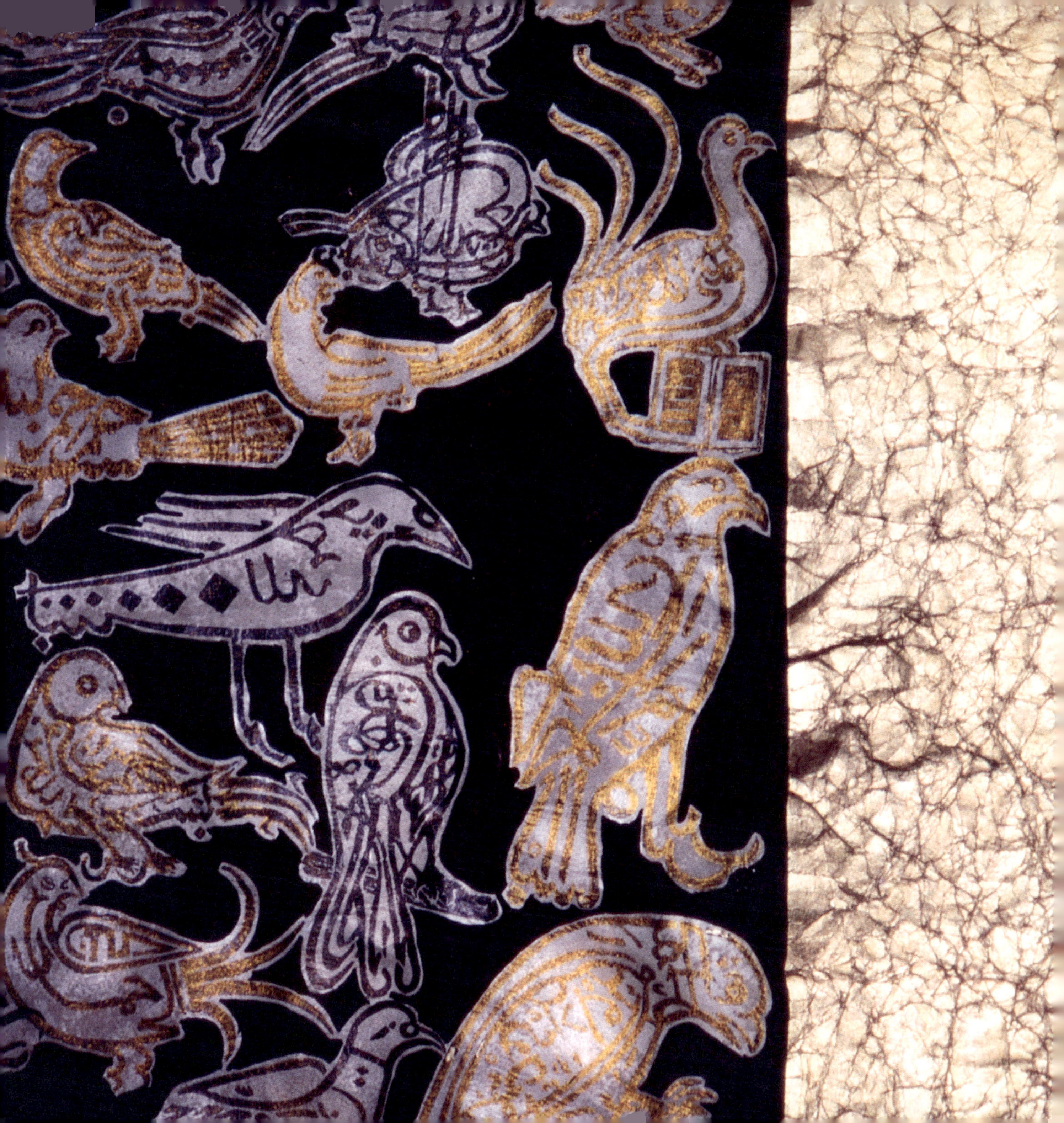

are obscure and whose history is fragmentary. On the motivation to twist text into images, Frederick de Jong of Utrecht University writes: 'Many images consist of mirror-image halves, a symbolic reference to the exoteric (*zahir*) and esoteric (*batin*) aspects of being.'

Day specifically chose to work with these images by collecting thirty examples from a wide variety of sources and recutting them onto wooden printing blocks. He printed them by hand, using relief printmaking, which is inevitably concerned with mirror images and symmetry. Once he had the thirty blocks of wood to do his monoprints, the series developed further. The latest one even included cut-out images of birds from old prints, which were collaged over his paintings. The early works were first exhibited in 1991 at the Jaliyan Gallery in London. Dick Davis (who translated Attar's poem for Penguin Books) honoured the gallery with his presence and acquired one of the works (page 16).

Different versions of the same series went to Iran – the Khaneh Honarmandan (House of Artists) in Tehran – and were exhibited in Beirut, Lebanon, at the Janine Rubeiz gallery. Later they were seen in London at the October Gallery and the Ismaili Centre.

Among the techniques, materials and ideas utilised in Day's interpretation is paper marbling. This purportedly Chinese method of decorating paper was practised at Bukhara during the 14th century, before continuing its journey along the Silk Road to Constantinople, then Venice and further west. It is often connected with mysticism. Day has extensively researched oriental marbling and has revitalised the integral technique where separate areas of patterns are juxtaposed using elaborate masking methods and are not collaged onto the sheet.[2]

Another feature that determined the use of monoprinting – where the blocks are applied by hand and not in a press – was anaphora. This is a literary device popular with Attar, where words or phrases are repeated and strung together like pearls. Day sees the repeated printing of the bird-image blocks, which are themselves made up of text, as a visual equivalent. In addition to the block printing, which is multiplied by reversing the image through printing onto very thin Nepalese tissue paper, the mostly Indian paper grounds are painted, stained, inscribed, sprinkled with multi-coloured mica, gilded and burnished, depending on the part of the poem chosen to be illustrated.

Day has no hesitation in labelling this series as 'illustrations of', which is anathema to most contemporary artists. His idea of interpretation is to accept the grandeur and seminal quality of a work as a given force and rework it, adding a gloss or nuance that reflects the time and context of its rebirth. These working methods are standard practice in theatre, music and architecture.

The printed image fascinates Day, who as a student worked with John Furnival at the Bath Academy of Art in the UK, going on to take postgraduate studies at the Slade School in London. He also lectured on fine art printmaking from 1973 till 2006. His work is in the collections of the British Library in London; The British Museum and the Victoria and Albert Museum in London; The Bibliothèque Nationale in Paris; the Museum of Modern Art in New York; and Prince Sadruddin Aga Khan is one of many private collectors.

I am very grateful to the poet and translators of Attar's book, Dick Davis and Afkham Darbandi, who have generously given us permission to use extracts of poems to illustrate the inspiration behind each work.[3]

ROSE ISSA

[1] The introduction of Attar's *The Conference of the Birds* (Penguin Classic edition, translated by Dick Davis and Afkham Darbandi, London 1984).

[2] *Integral Marbling*, Graham Day, Bibliotheque Municipale de Rennes, 1990.

[3] Farid ud-Din Attar, *The Conference of the Birds*, transl. by Afkham Darbandi and Dick Davis, Penguin Classics, 1984.

  Detail of the monoprinted painting on pages 30–31

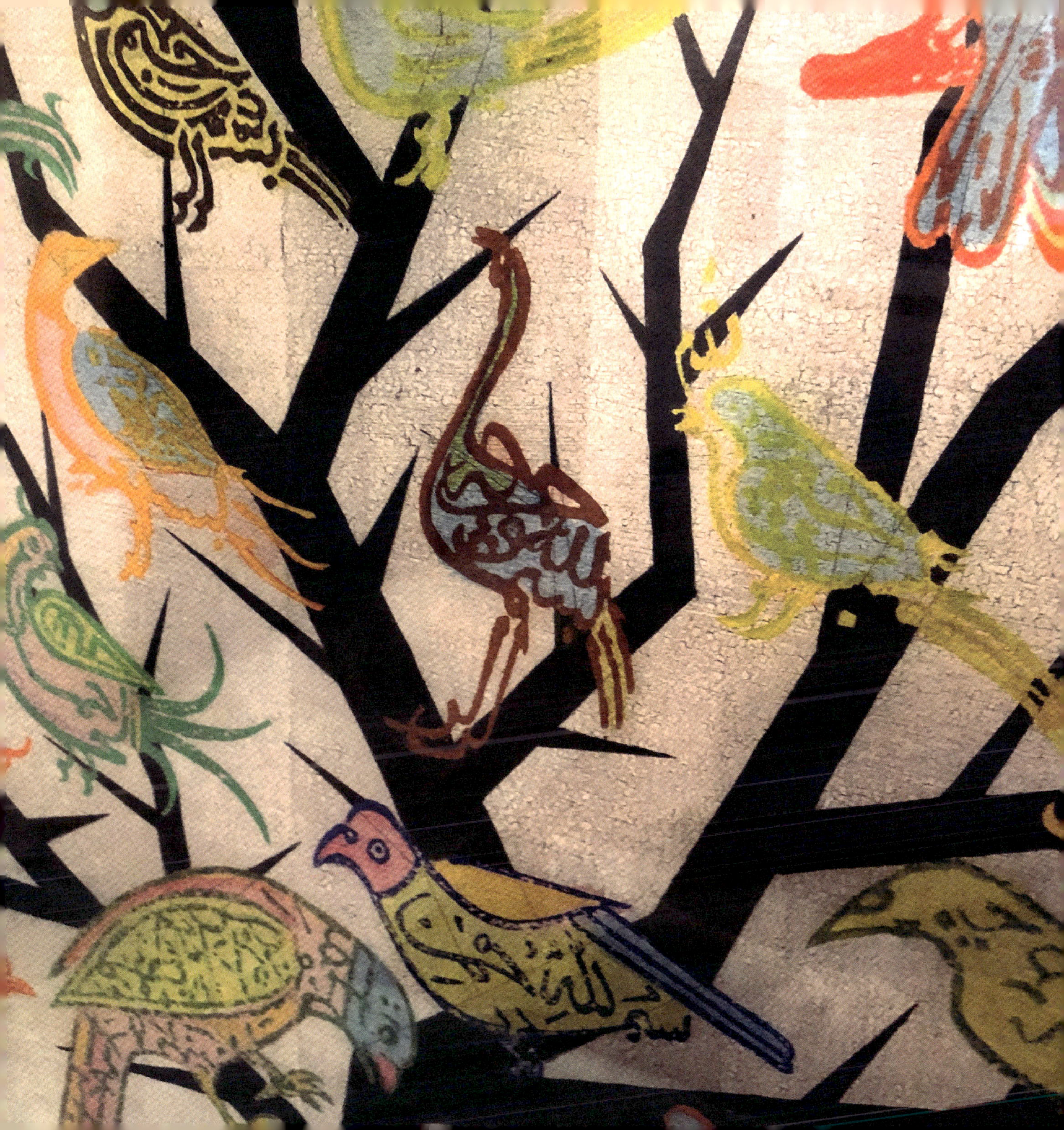

ARTIST STATEMENT

In the 1960s, at Bath Academy of Art in the UK, I met Dom Sylvester Houédard and John Furnival, artists and teachers who introduced me to concrete poetry, now known as visual poetry. They showed me that letters and words could be combined in various ways. Being slightly dyslexic and visually sensitive, I had always had a curious relationship with reading. Looking at words on a page, I was always struck by the shapes of the letters; I wasn't so interested in what the words meant, it was the shapes that held my attention and got me making pictures using my old typewriter.

At the Academy there were wood and metal type forms: you could pick them up, consider them back to front and upside down. Letters were objects, their meaning only an aspect of their shape. Studying philology at the Academy showed me that, historically, text and image had been treated differently, pages of text separated by pages of illustrations. So, when I encountered Arabic zoomorphic calligraphy – words in the shape of animals – what I saw was an obvious delight. I couldn't read the words; I was told that they were Islamic invocations. And when I met Rose Issa, she introduced me to Persian culture, and to a well-known 12th-century poem *The Conference of the Birds* by Farid ud-Din Attar: it was the obvious subject to be illustrated using the zoomorphic bird images.

I located and chose thirty examples of the zoomorphic birds, drawing them onto blocks, cutting them out, and printing them down by hand. I used the blocks like large rubber stamps, printing onto lovely deckle-edged sheets of Nepalese paper. I always insisted that these pictures should be accompanied by the part of the poem that had inspired me. It was easy to choose the translation from Persian to English made by Afkham Darbandi and Dick Davis, published by Penguin Classics, over that of Peter Avery. The former is rendered in alliterative rhyme:

Give up the intellect for love and see
In one brief moment all eternity

which is the same metre used in the Rupert the Bear annual books for children:

Just look what I have, Rupert cried,
And Mr Bear turned in surprise.

Rupert the Bear was a familiar presence for English children from 1920 and is still going strong today. The rhyming couplets in both texts cry out to be read aloud, where different accents and emphasis in sound can be applied to the mere words in the same way that the words can be accented with shapes and colours.

So, when you look at these pictures, read out the poem aloud.

GRAHAM DAY
London, summer 2024

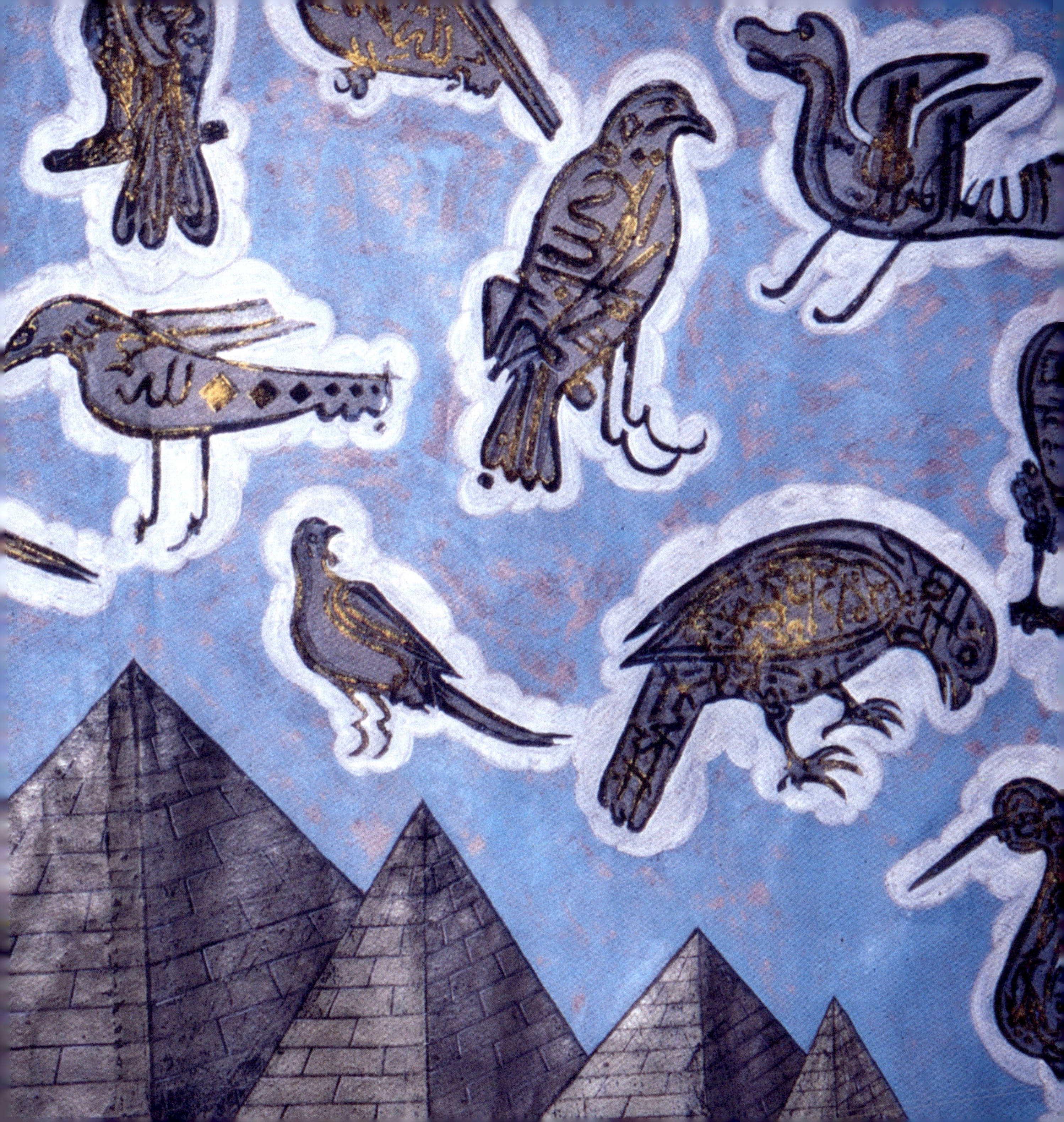

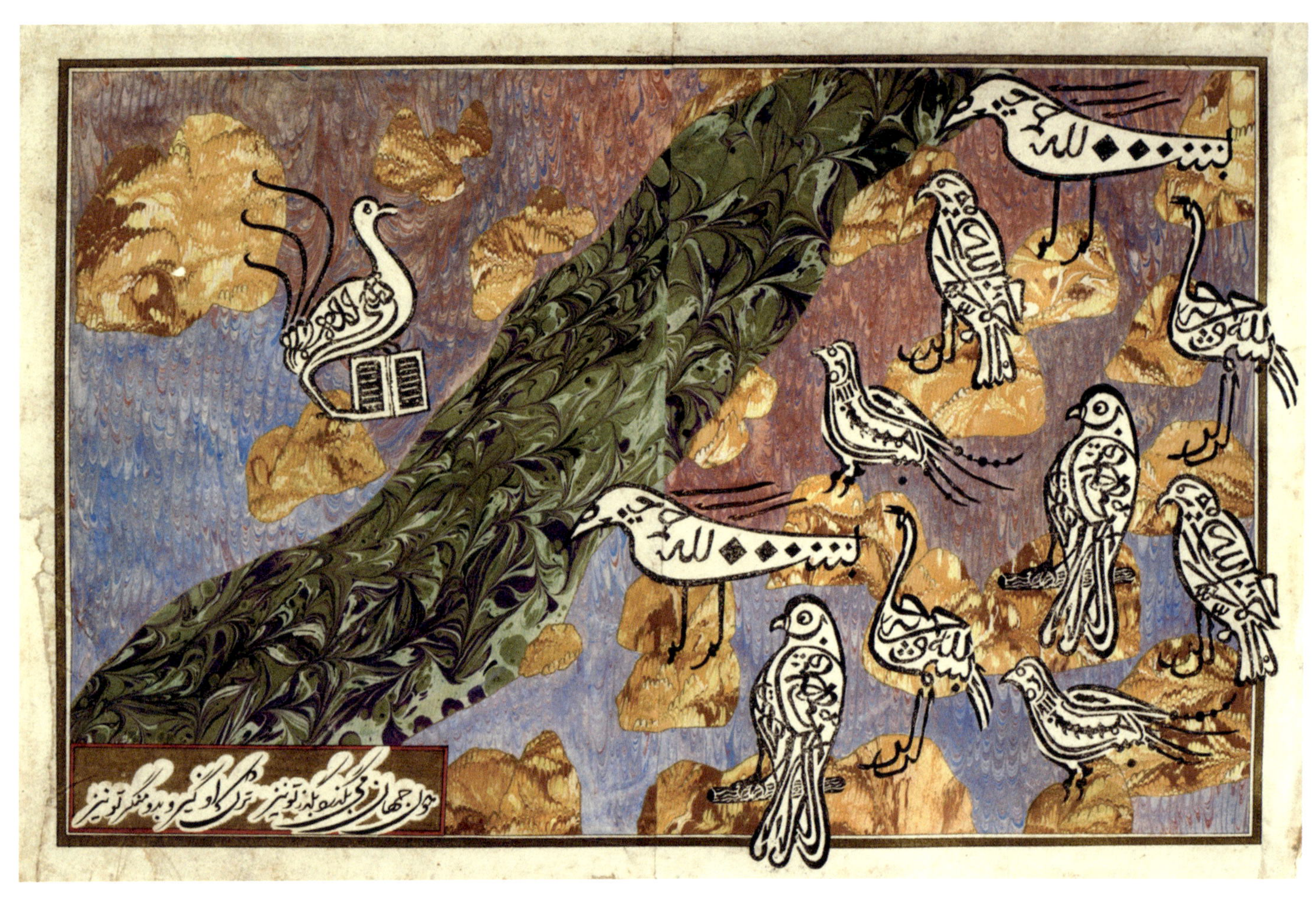

10   Monoprint and marbling on handmade Indian paper, 53 x 83 cm, 1991. Private collection

'Why do you waste your life in slothful sleep?
Rise up, for there is nothing you can keep;
What will it profit you to comprehend
The present world when it must have an end?'

Give up the intellect for love and see
In one brief moment all eternity;
Break nature's frame, be resolute and brave,
Then rest at peace in Unity's black cave [...]

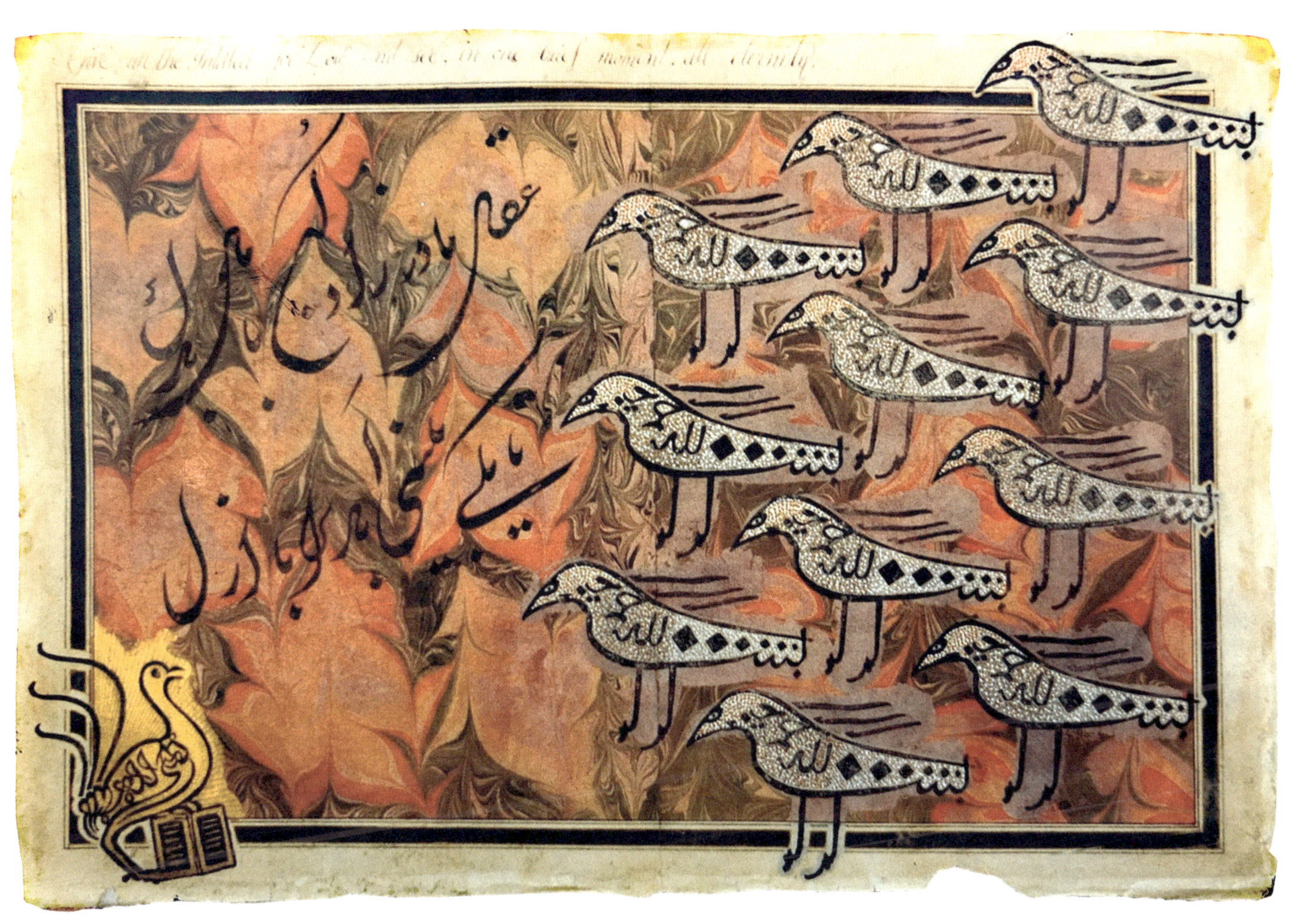

Monoprint and marbling and gold on handmade Indian paper, 53 x 83 cm, 1991. Private collection

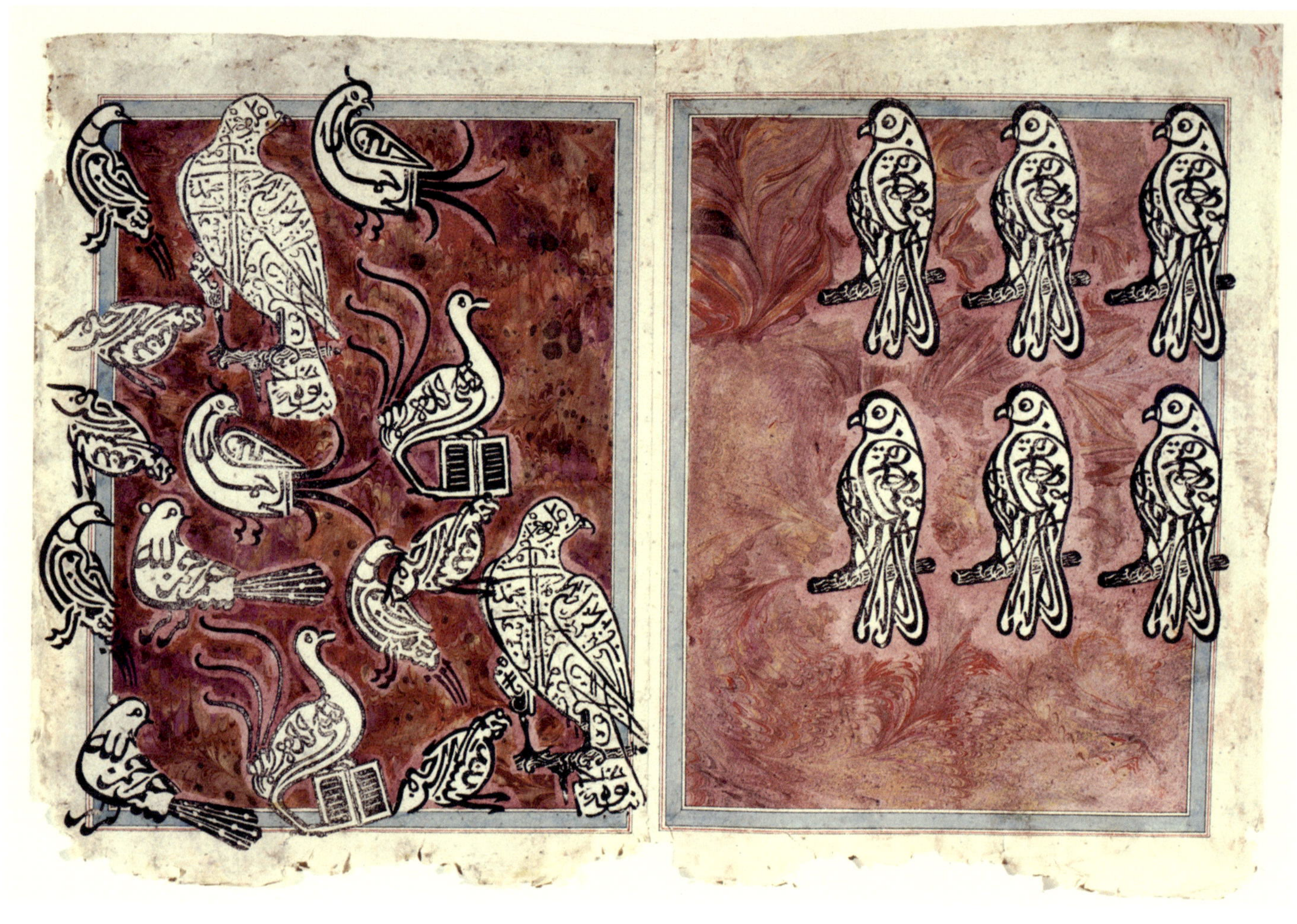

Whoever can evade the Self transcends
This world and as a lover he ascends.
Set free your soul; impatient of delay,
Step out along our sovereign's royal Way.

  Monoprint and marbling on handmade Indian paper, 53 x 83 cm, 1991. Collection of The British Museum, London

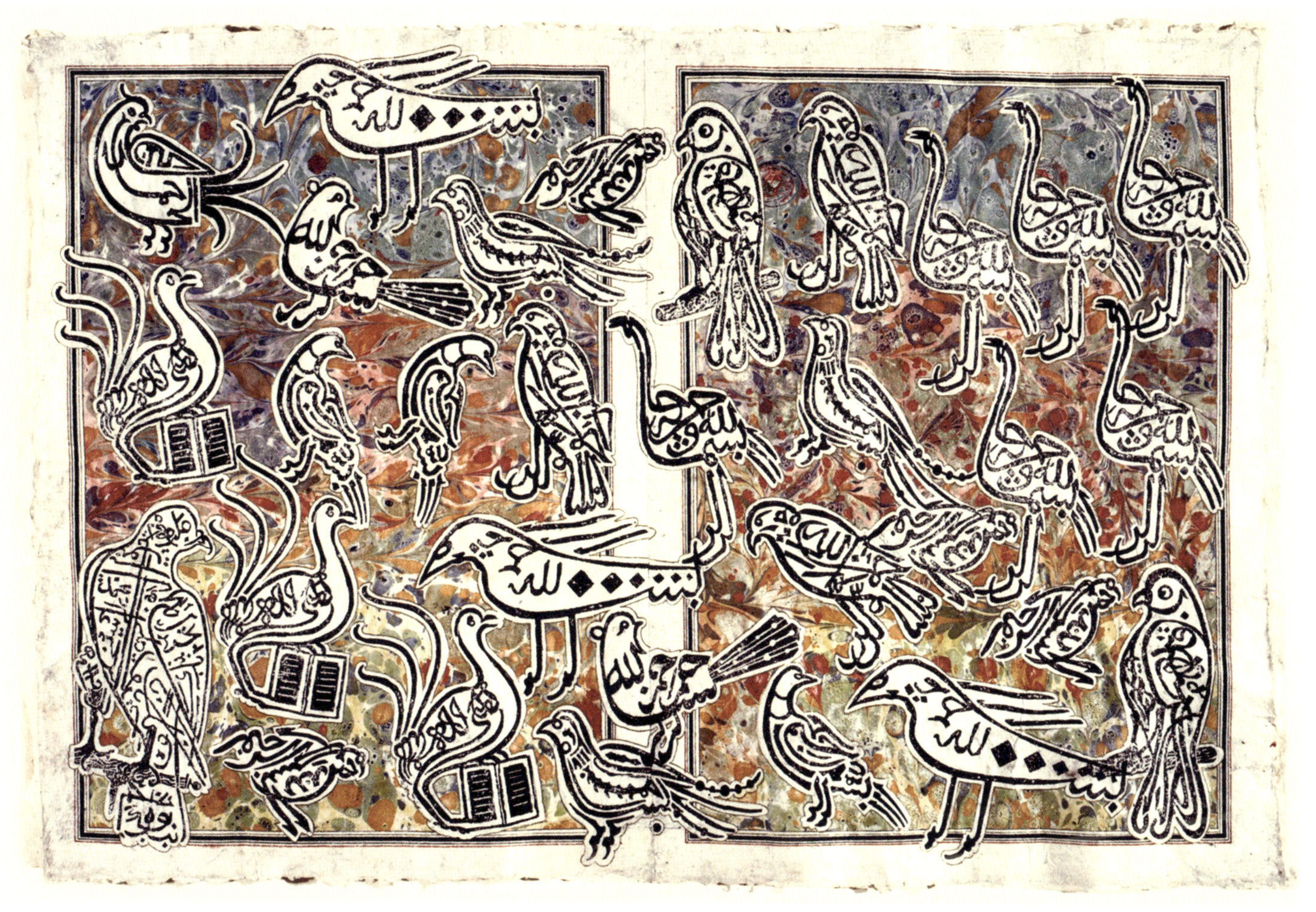

The world's birds gathered for their conference
And said: 'Our constitution makes no sense.
All nations in the world require a King;
How is it that we alone have no such thing?

Monoprint and marbling on handmade Indian paper, 53 x 83 cm, 1991. Collection of The British Museum, London

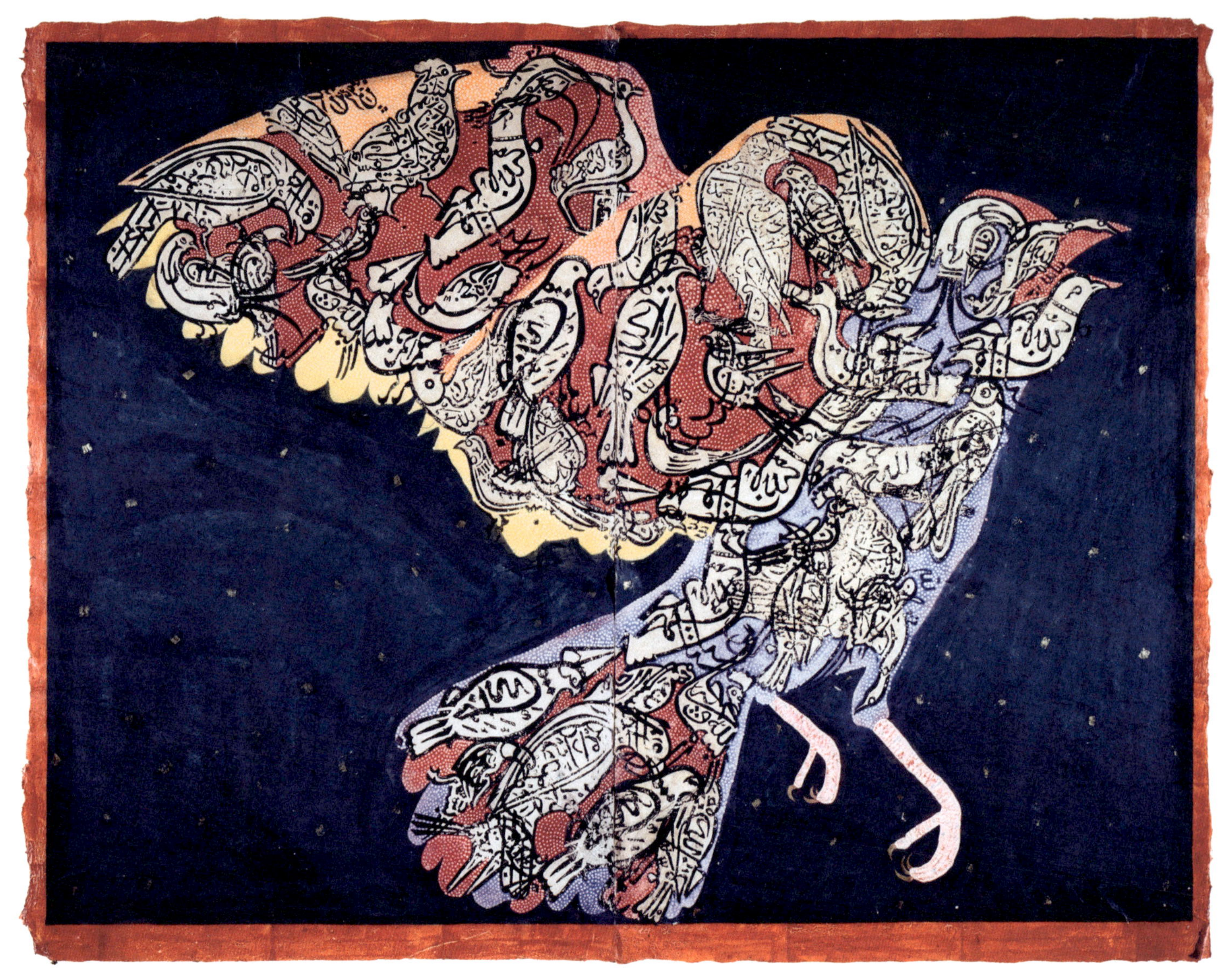

  Monoprint and gouache on handmade Indian paper, 83 x 106 cm, 1991. Collection, Dick Davis, USA

They see the Simorgh – at themselves they stare,
And see a second Simorgh stand there;
They look at both and see the two are one,
That this is that, that this, the goal is won.

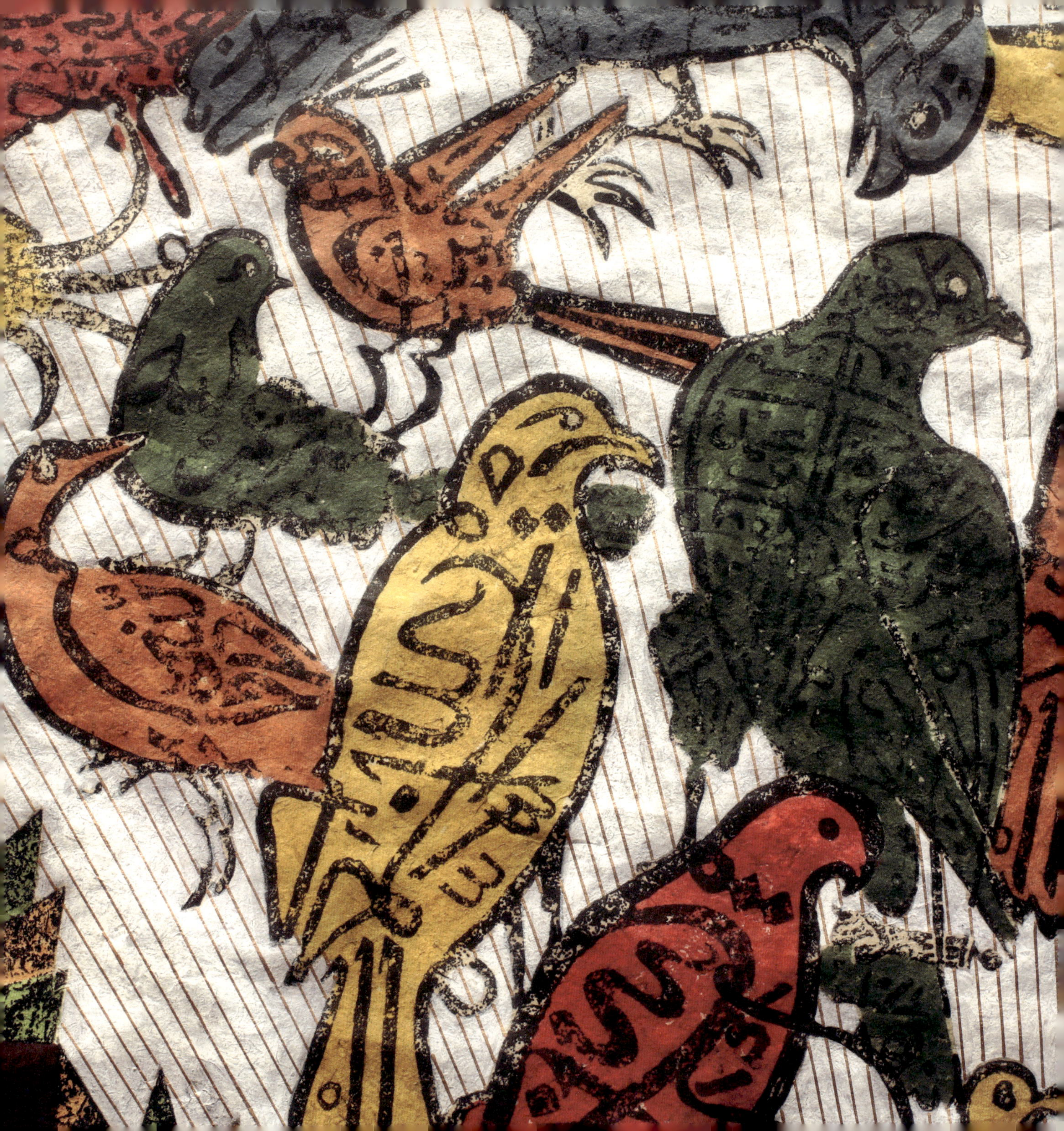

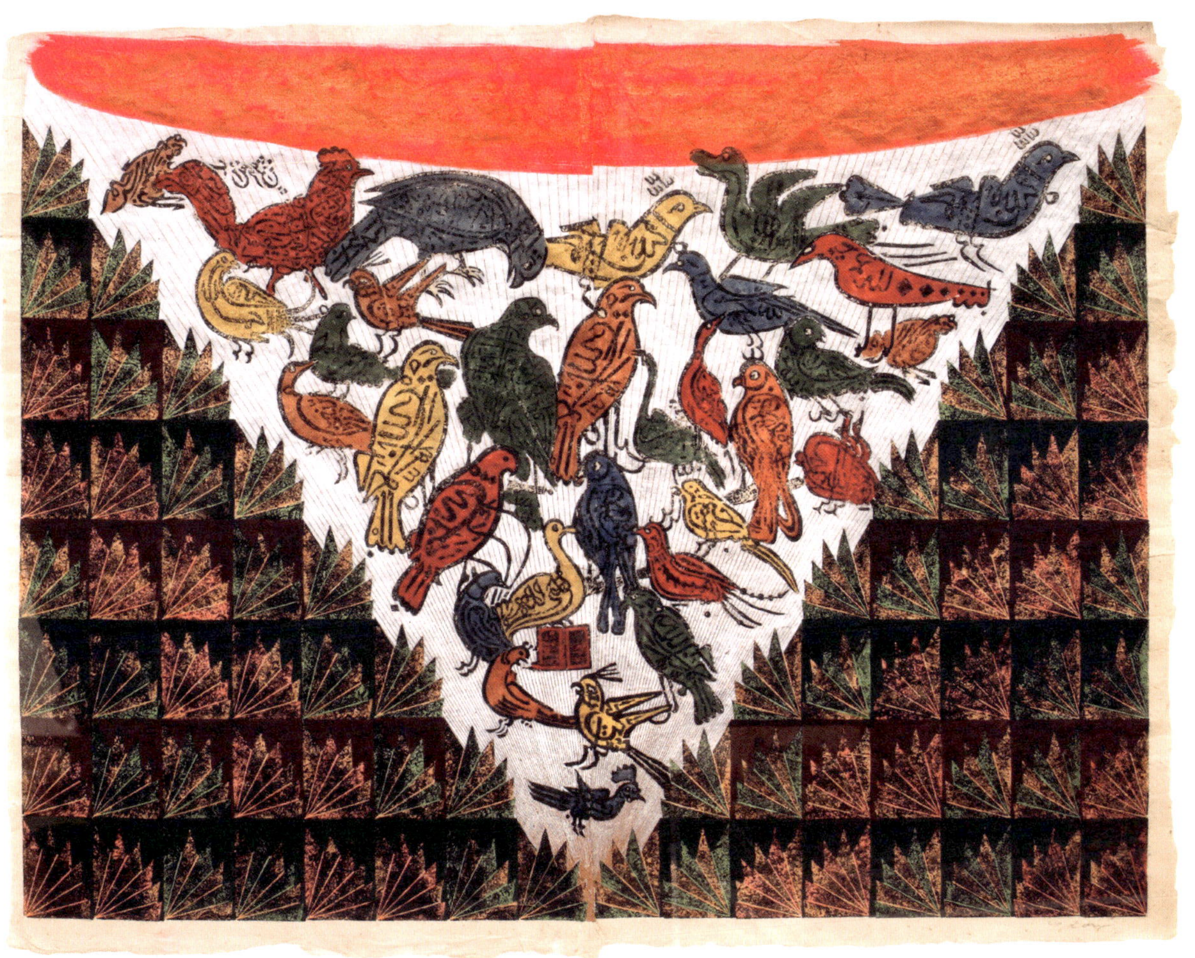

And Panic spread among the birds, they feared
The endless desolation which appeared.
They clung together in a huddling crowd,
Drew in their wings and wailed aloud.

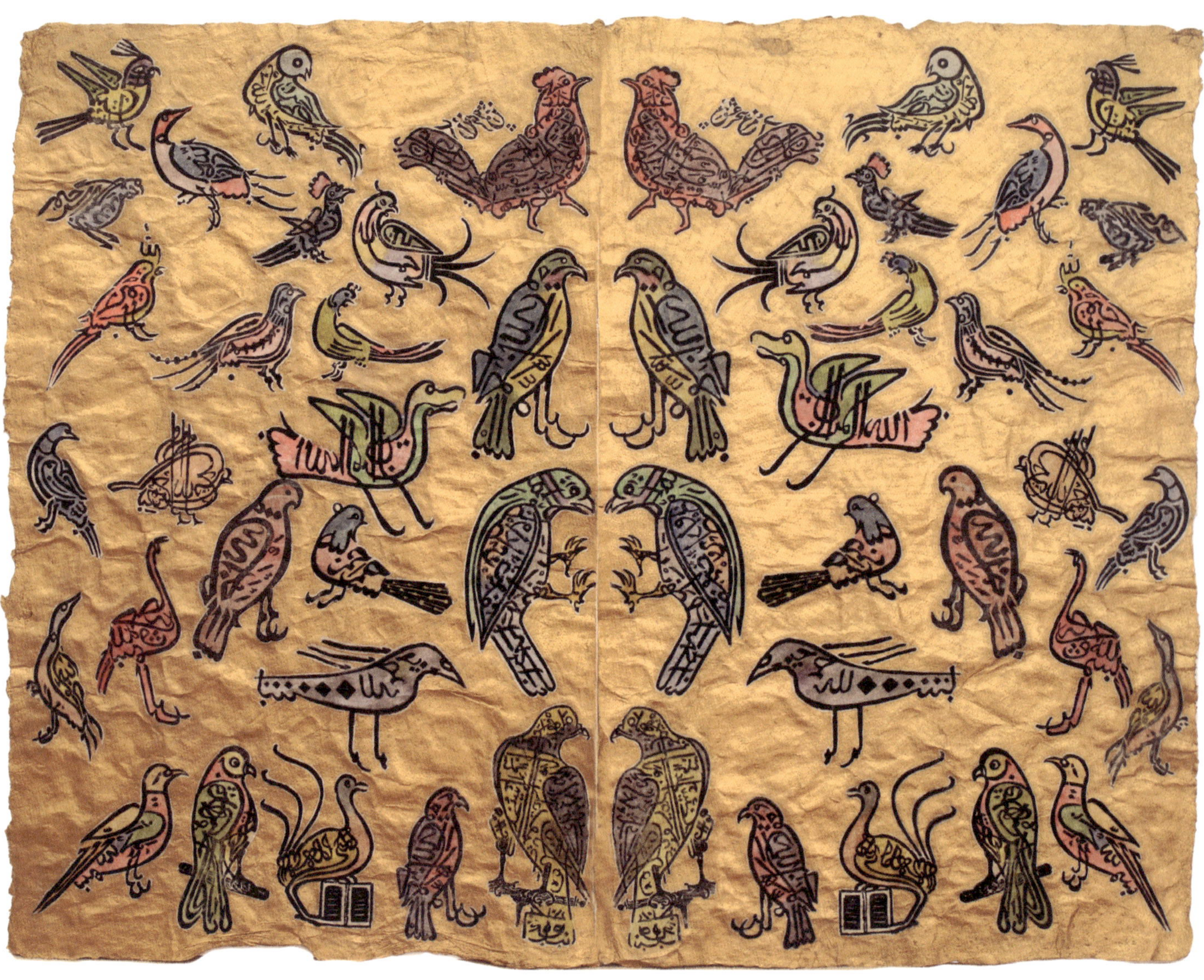

 Monoprint and gouache on handmade Indian paper, 83 x 106 cm, 1991. Private collection, London. Details pages 20–21

I am a mirror set before your eyes,
And all who come before my splendour see
Themselves, their own unique reality [...]

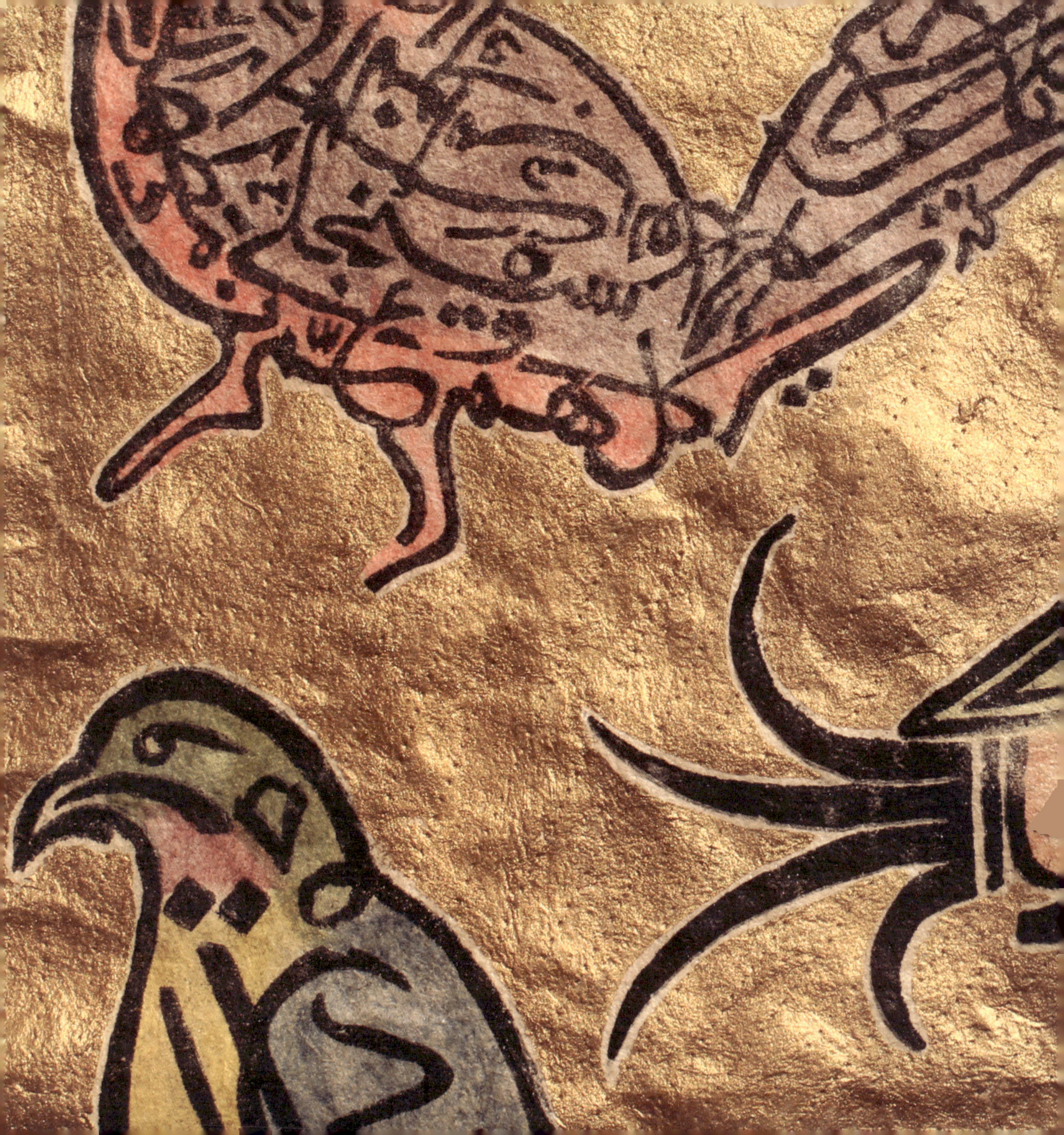

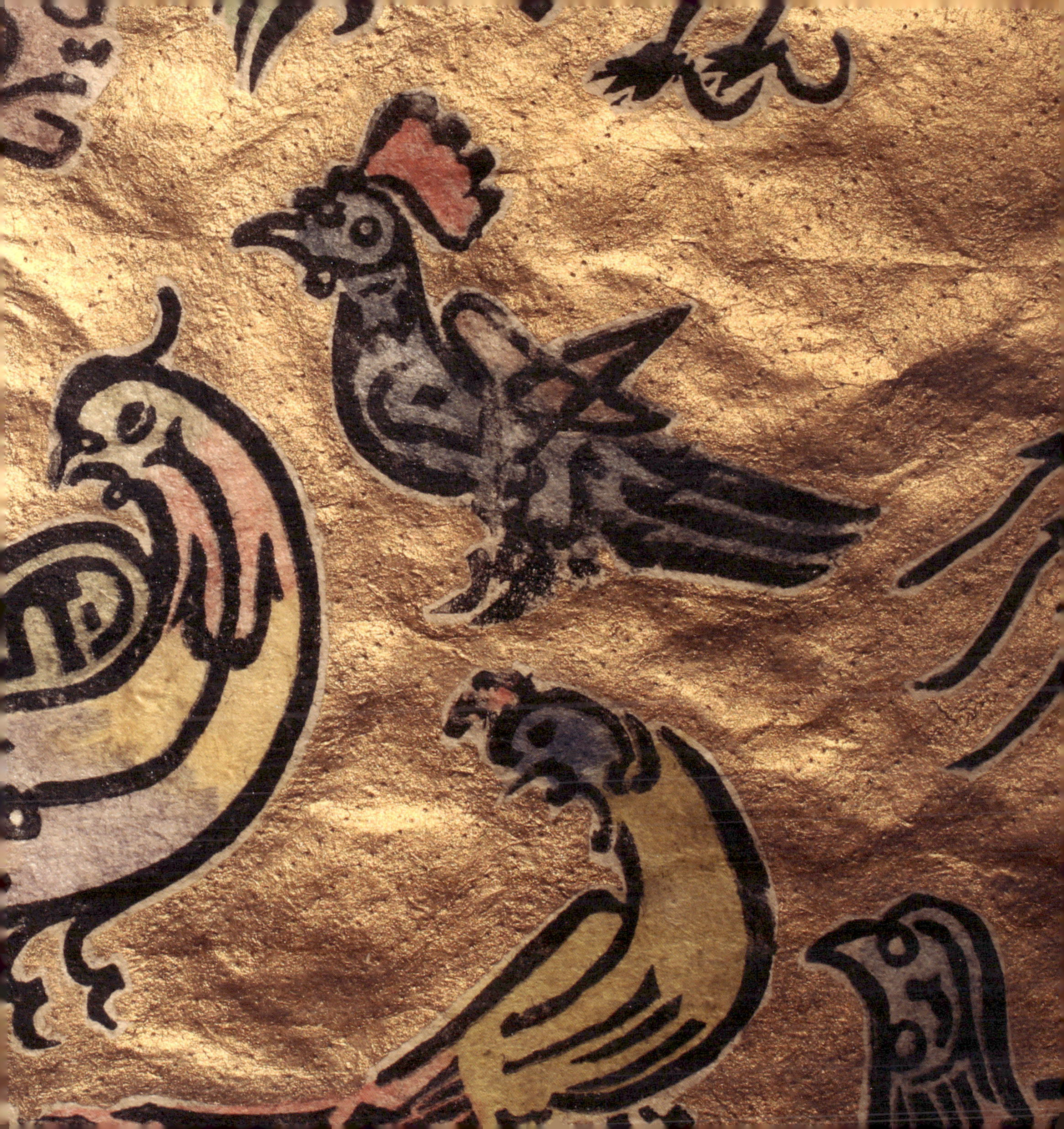

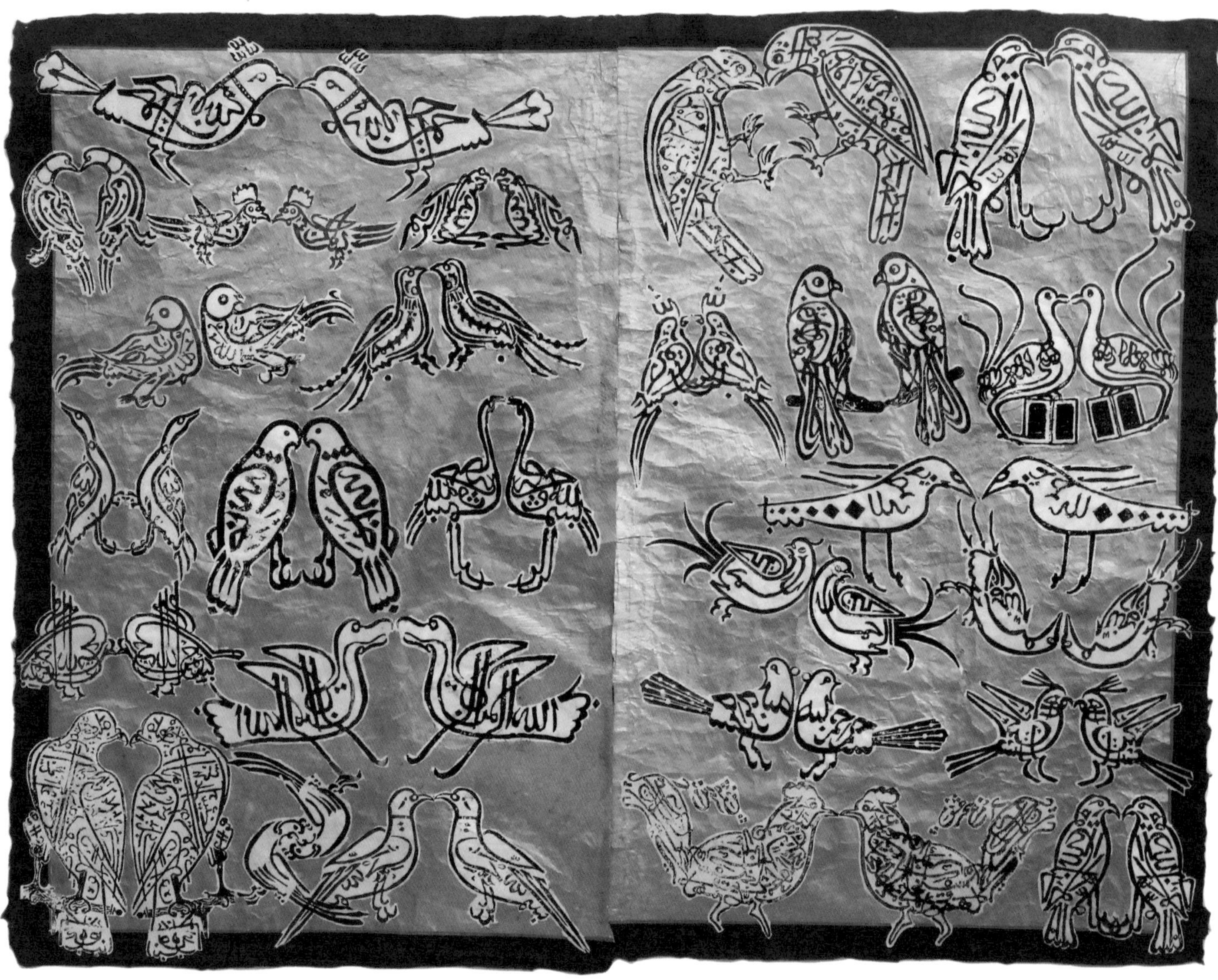

 Monoprint and gold on handmade Indian paper, 83 x 106 cm, 1991. Private collection, London

Though you have struggled, wandered, travelled far
It is you yourselves you see and what you are.

Their life came from that close, insistent sun
And in its vivid rays they shone as one.
There in the Simorgh's radiant face they saw
Themselves, the Simorgh of the world – with awe.

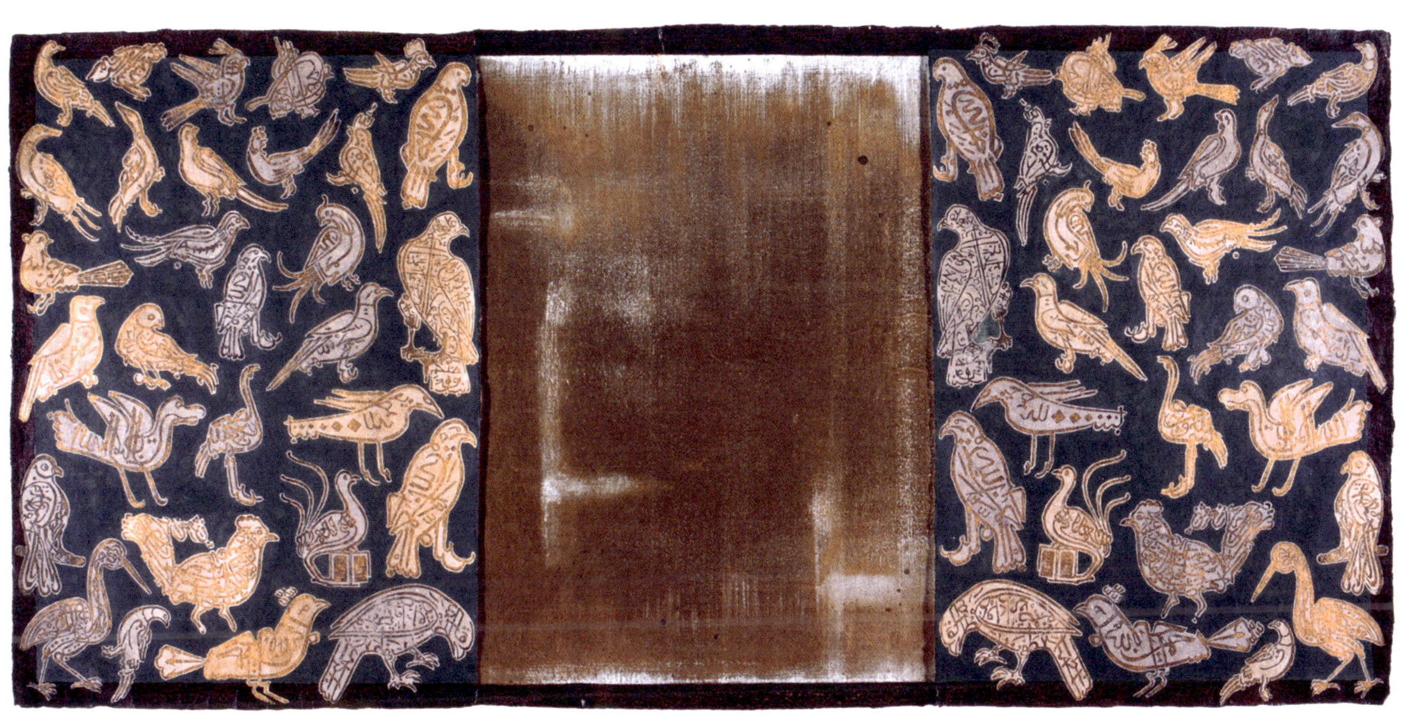

Monoprint, acrylic and gold on handmade Indian paper, 83 x 159 cm, 1992. Private collection, Germany

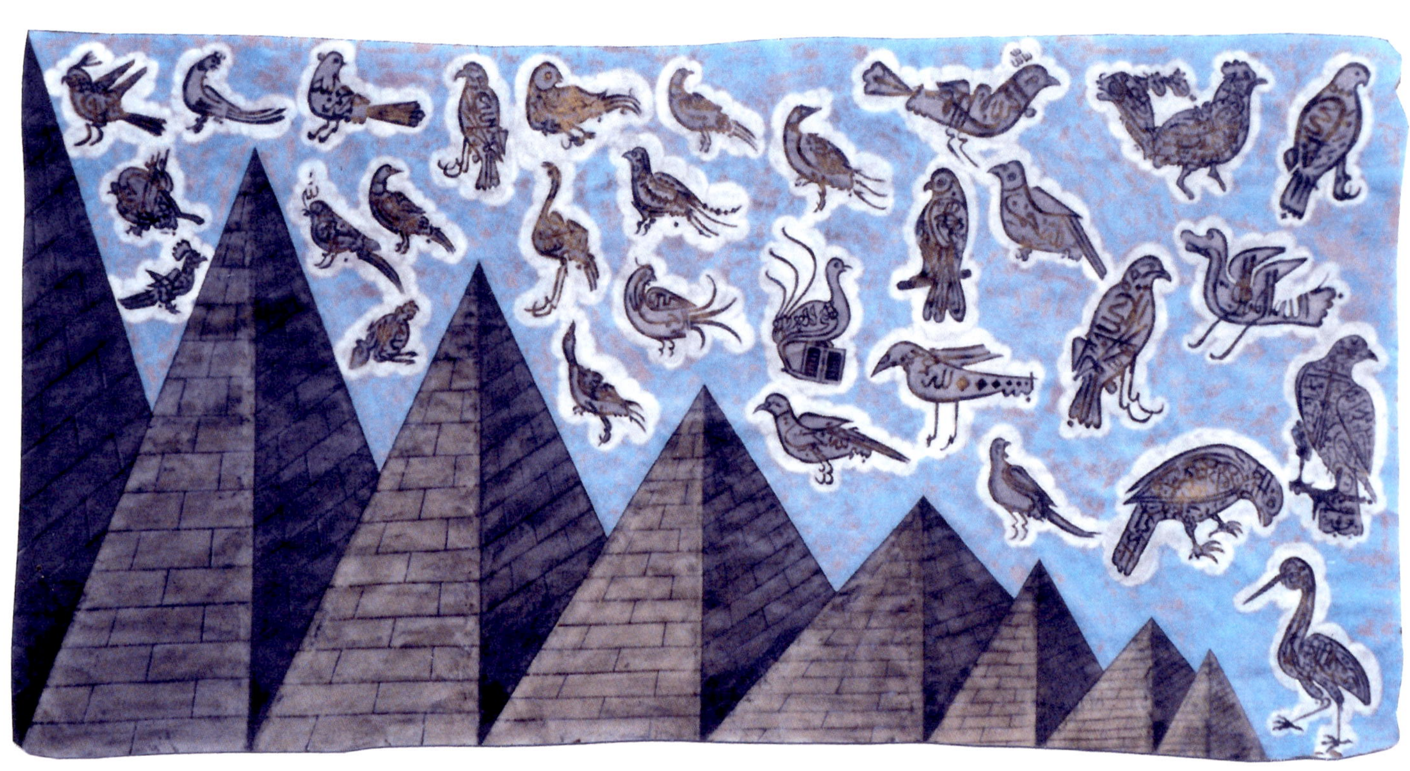

28   Monoprint and acrylic on handmade Indian paper, triptych, 83 x 159 cm, 1992. Collection World Bank, Washington DC, USA

'Before we reach our goal,' the hoopoe said
'The journey's seven valleys lie ahead;
How far this is the world has never learned,
For no one who has gone there has returned'

The world's birds gathered for their conference
And said: 'Our constitution makes no sense.
All nations in the world require a King;
How is it that we alone have no such thing?'

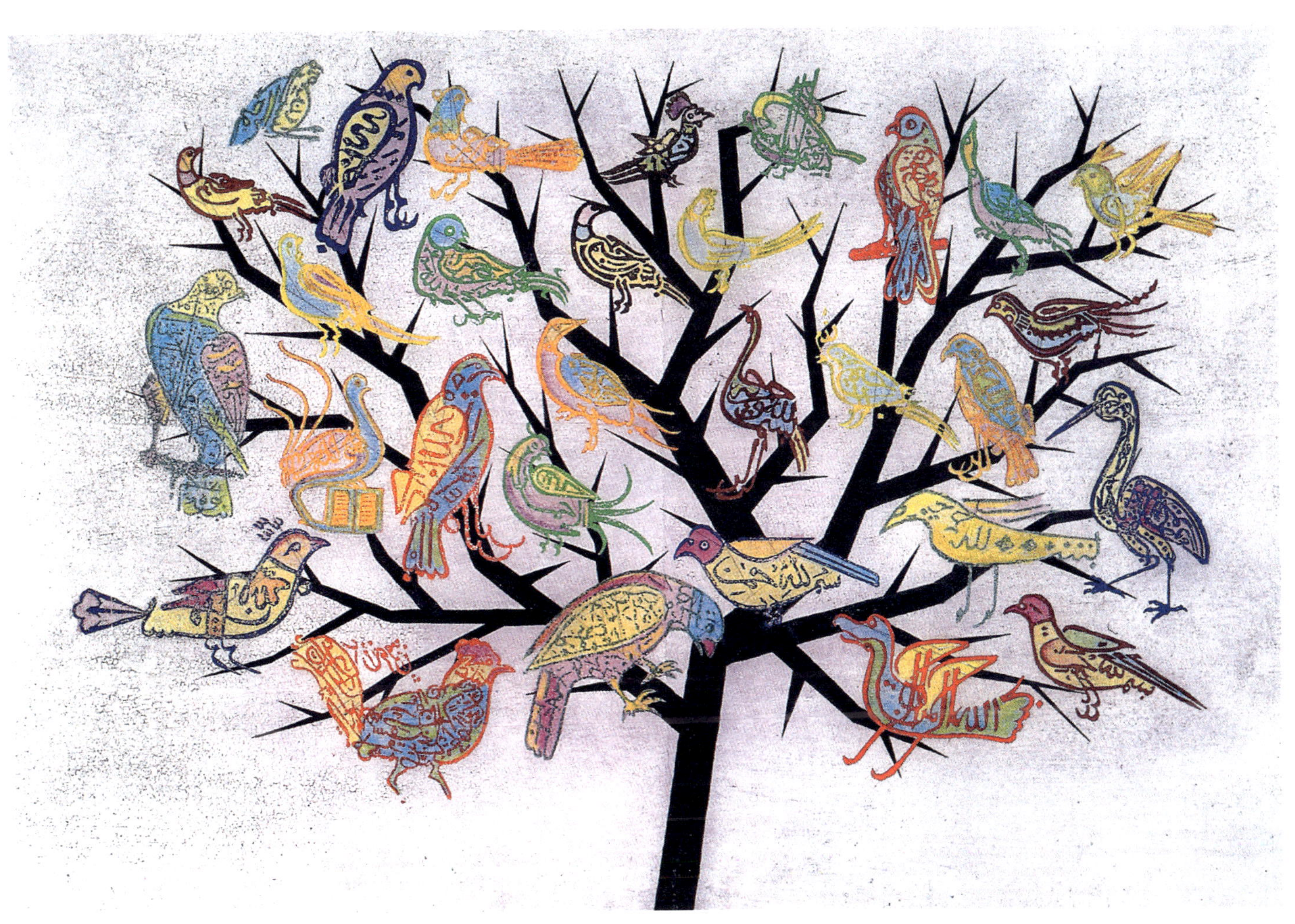

Monoprint and gouache on handmade Indian paper, 83 x 106 cm, 1999. Private collection, Nice, France

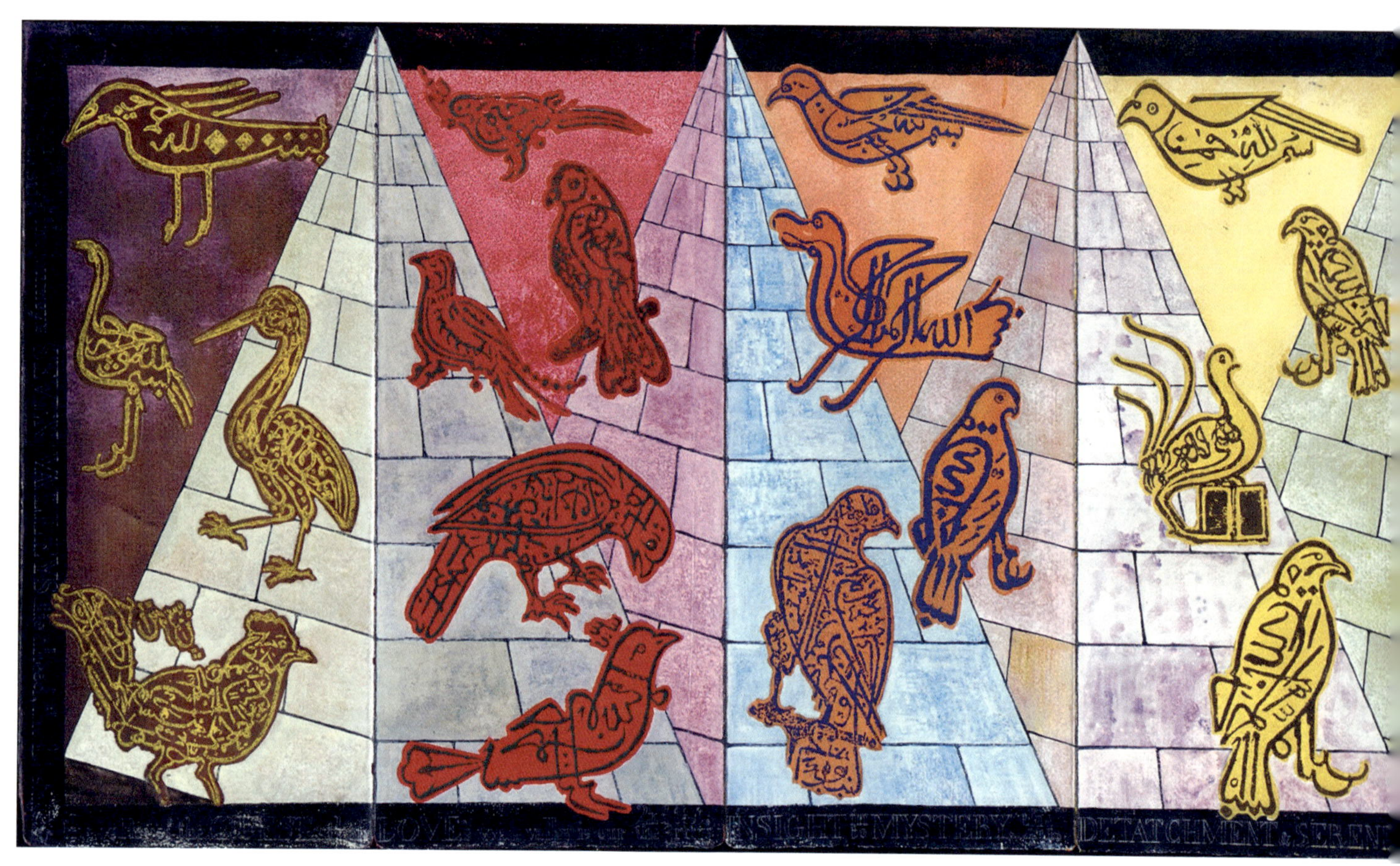

LOVE
INSIGHT & MYSTERY
DETATCHMENT & SEREN

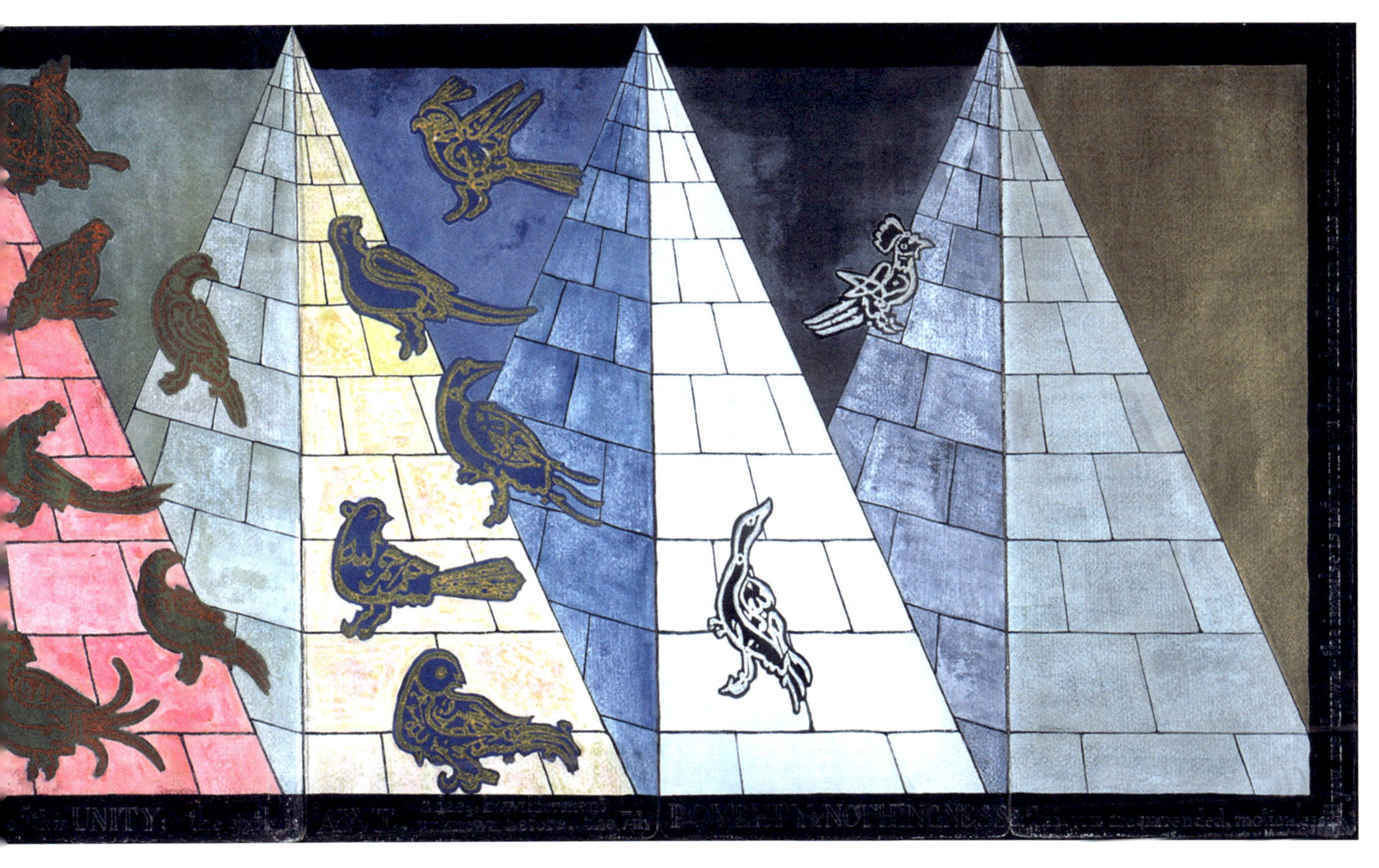

Though you traversed the Valleys' depths and fought
With all the dangers that the journey brought [...]

Monoprint and mixed media on paper, 83 x 159 cm, 2002. Private collection

If You would glimpse the beauty we revere
Look in your heart – its image will appear.
Make of your heart a looking-glass and see
Reflected there the Friend's nobility [...]

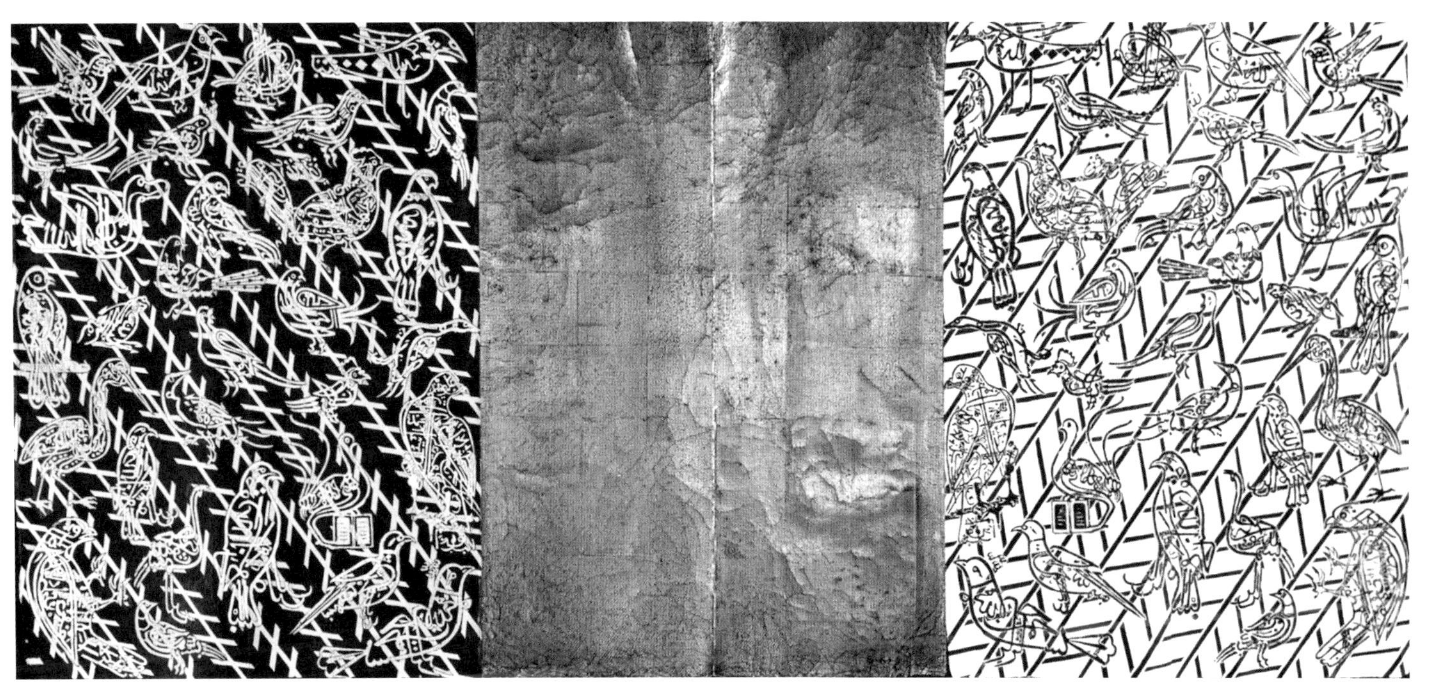

Monoprint, mixed media and silver leaf on handmade paper, 83 x 159 cm, 2013. Private collection

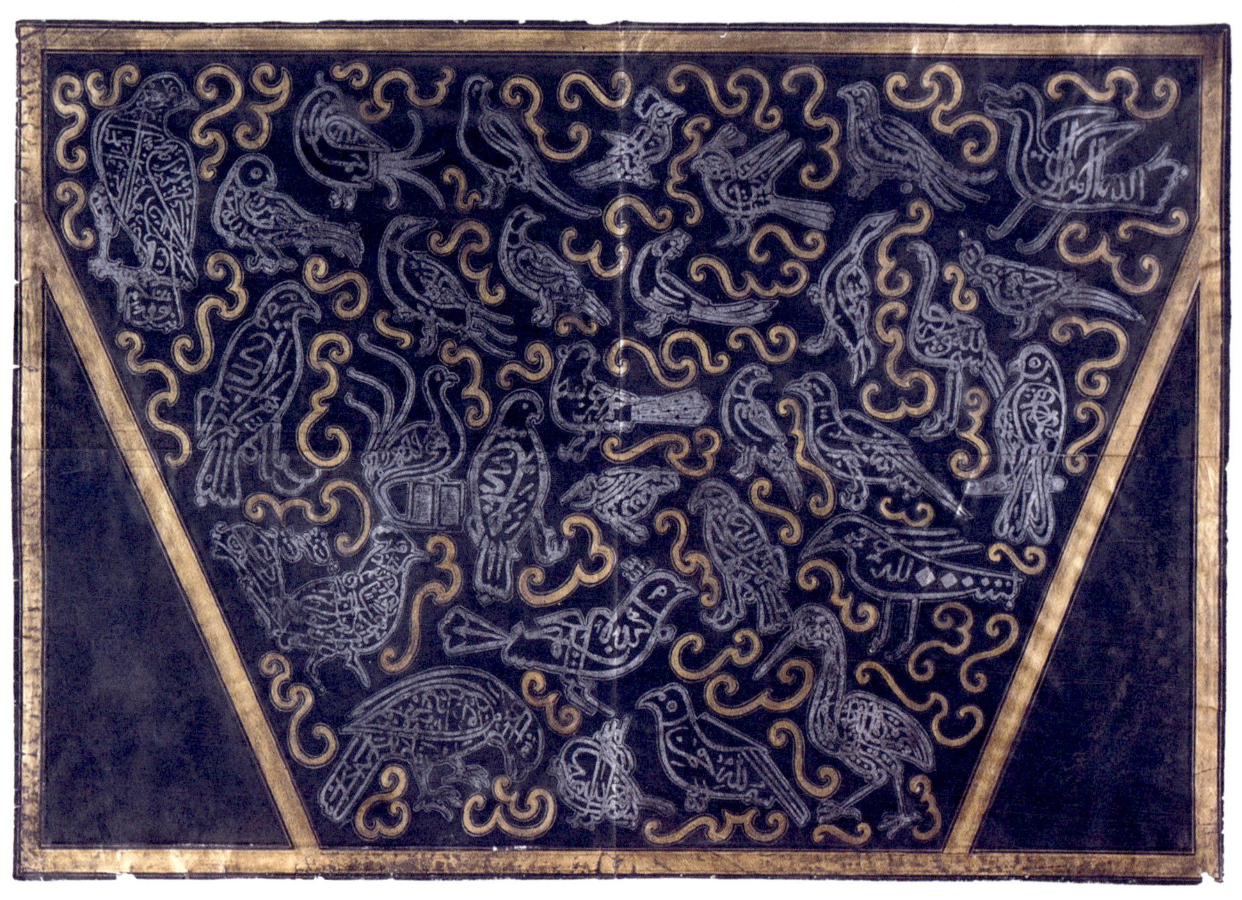

It was in China, late one moonless night,
The Simorgh first appeared to mortal sight –
He let a feather float down through the air,
And rumours of its fame spread everywhere [...]

Monoprint, ink and gold, 83 x 106 cm, 2001. Private collection

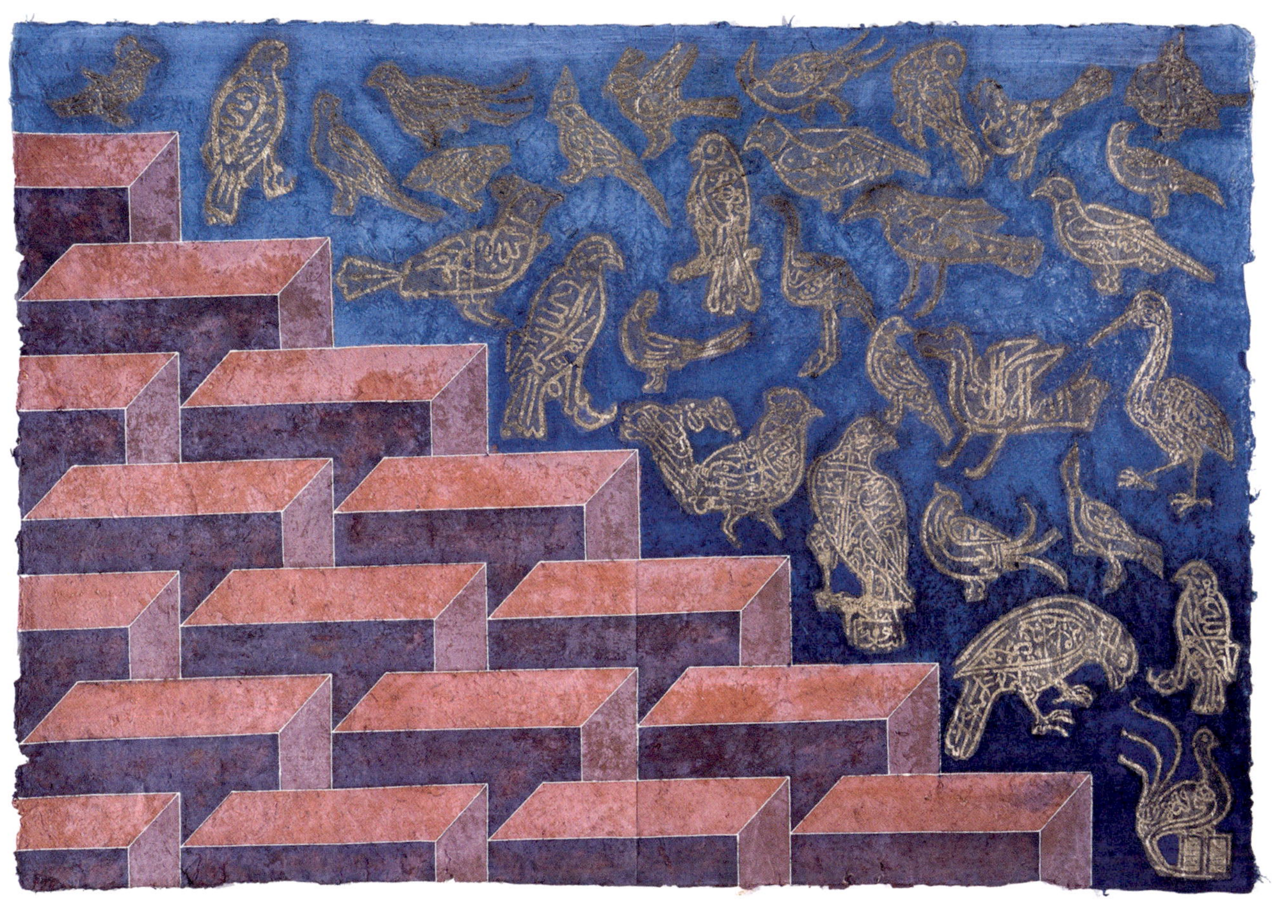

'Before we reach our goal,' the hoopoe said
'The journey's seven valleys lie ahead;
How far this is the world has never learned,
For no one who has gone there has returned [...]

Monoprint and mixed media on handmade paper, 83 x 106 cm, 2001. Private collection

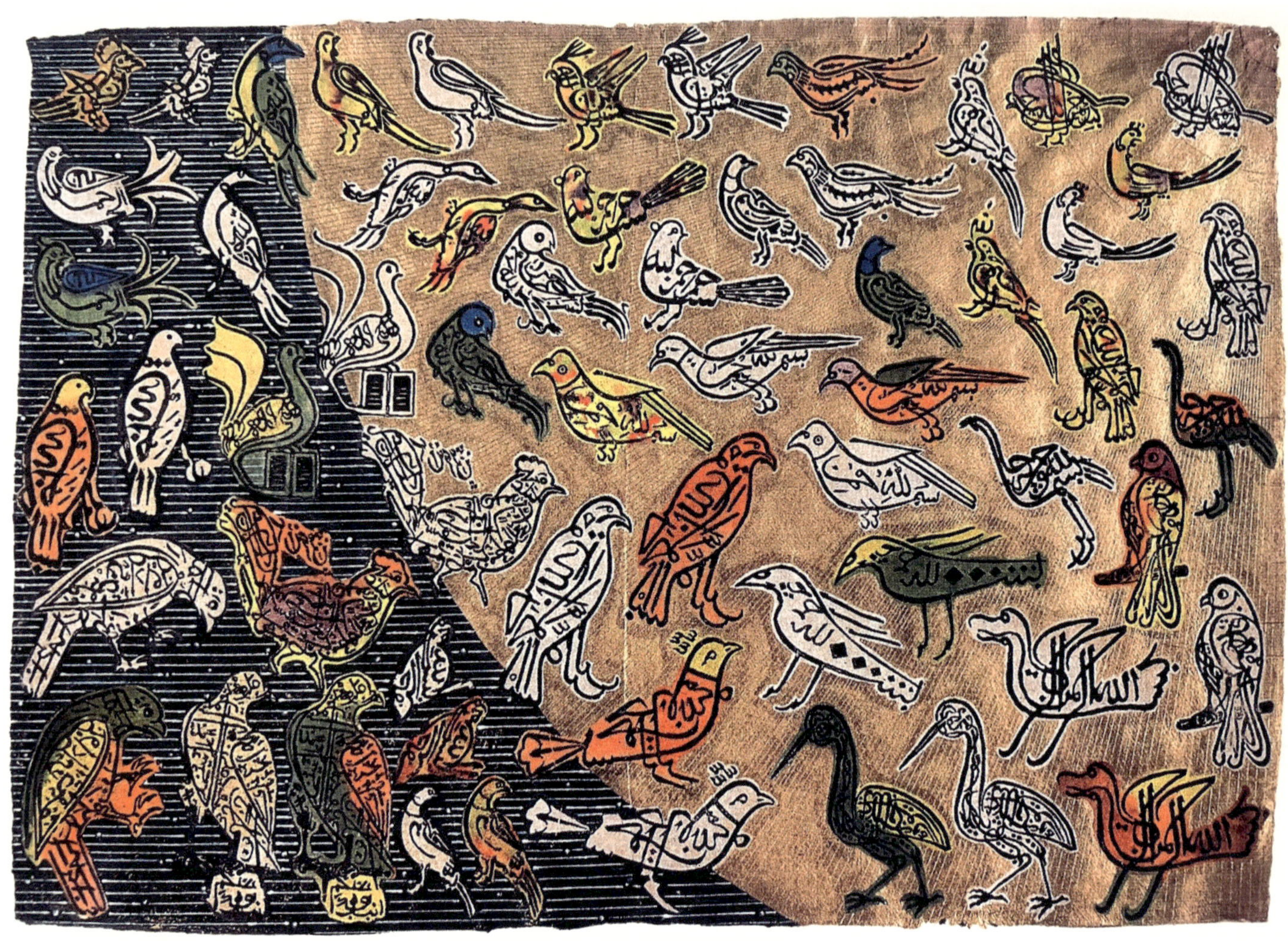

Monoprint, acrylic and gold, 83 x 106 cm, 2001. Private collection

If thousands were to die here, they would be
One drop of dew absorbed within the sea;
A hundred thousand fools would be as one
Brief atom's shadow in the blazing sun [...]

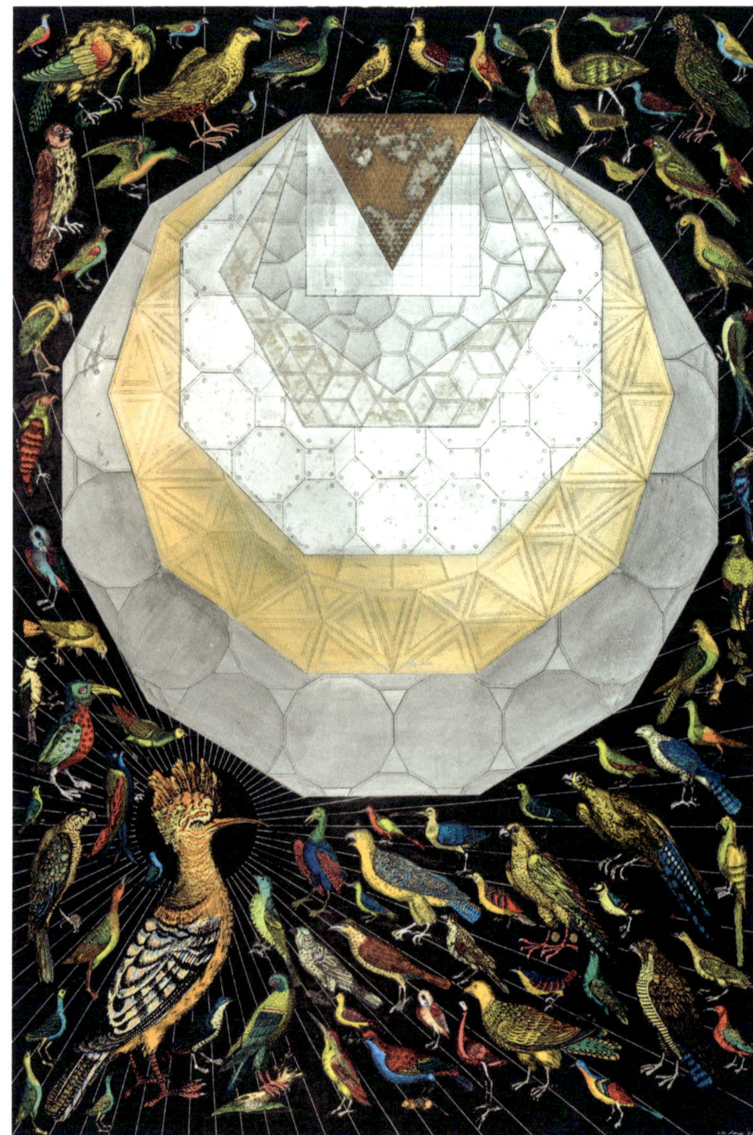

The hoopoe as their chief was hailed and crowned –
Huge flocks of birds in homage gathered round;
A hundred thousand birds assembled there,
Making a monstrous shadow in the air.

     Monoprint, mixed media and collages on handmade Indian paper, 110 x 80 cm, 2007. Collection of the artist

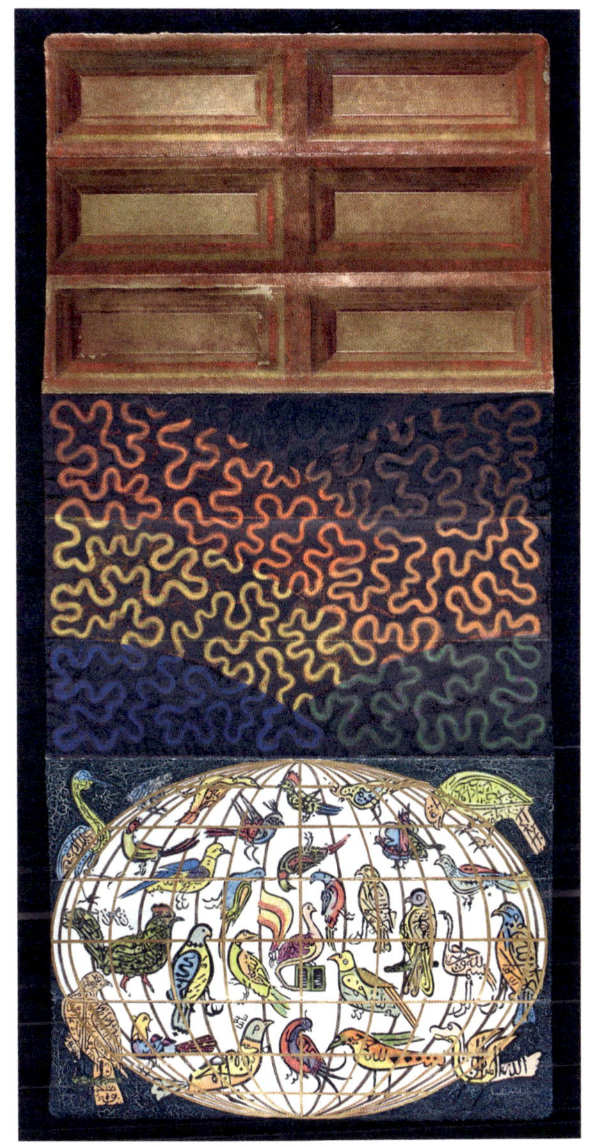

While you still travel in your worldly state,
You cannot pass beyond this glorious gate.
Why do you waste your life in slothful sleep?
Rise up, for there is nothing you can keep.

How can you reach the Simorgh's splendid court?
First find its gateway, and the sun long-sought,
Erupts through clouds; when victory is won,
Your sight knows nothing but the blinding sun.

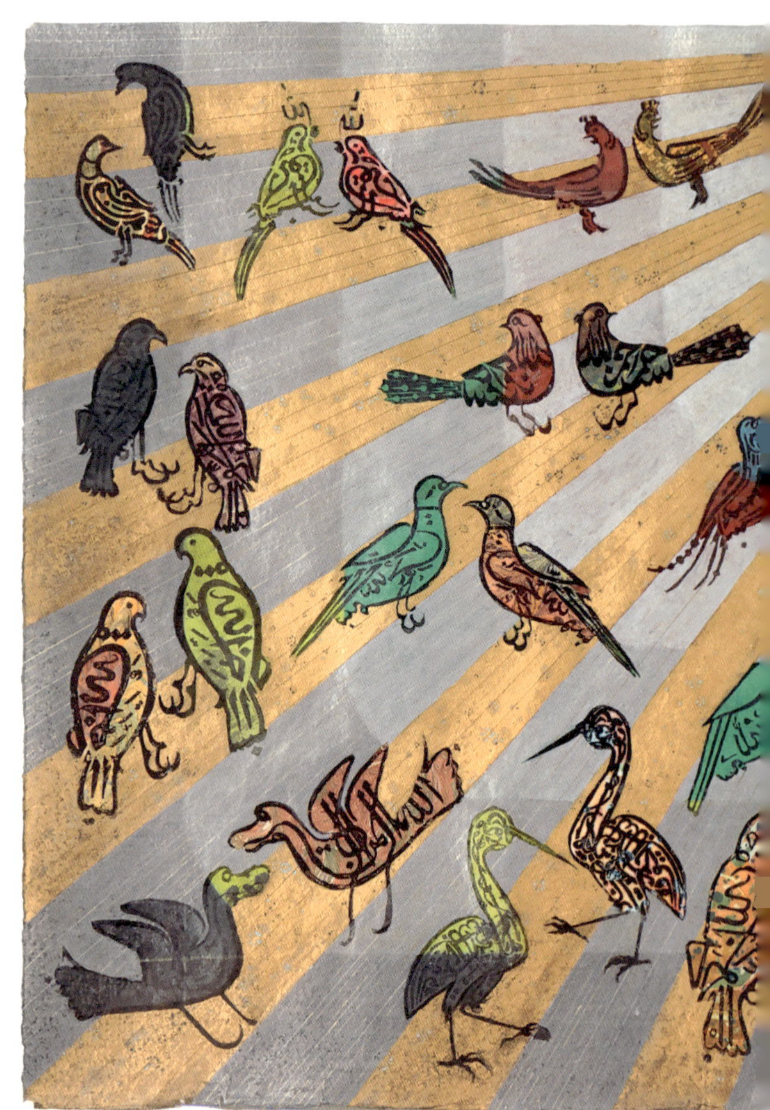

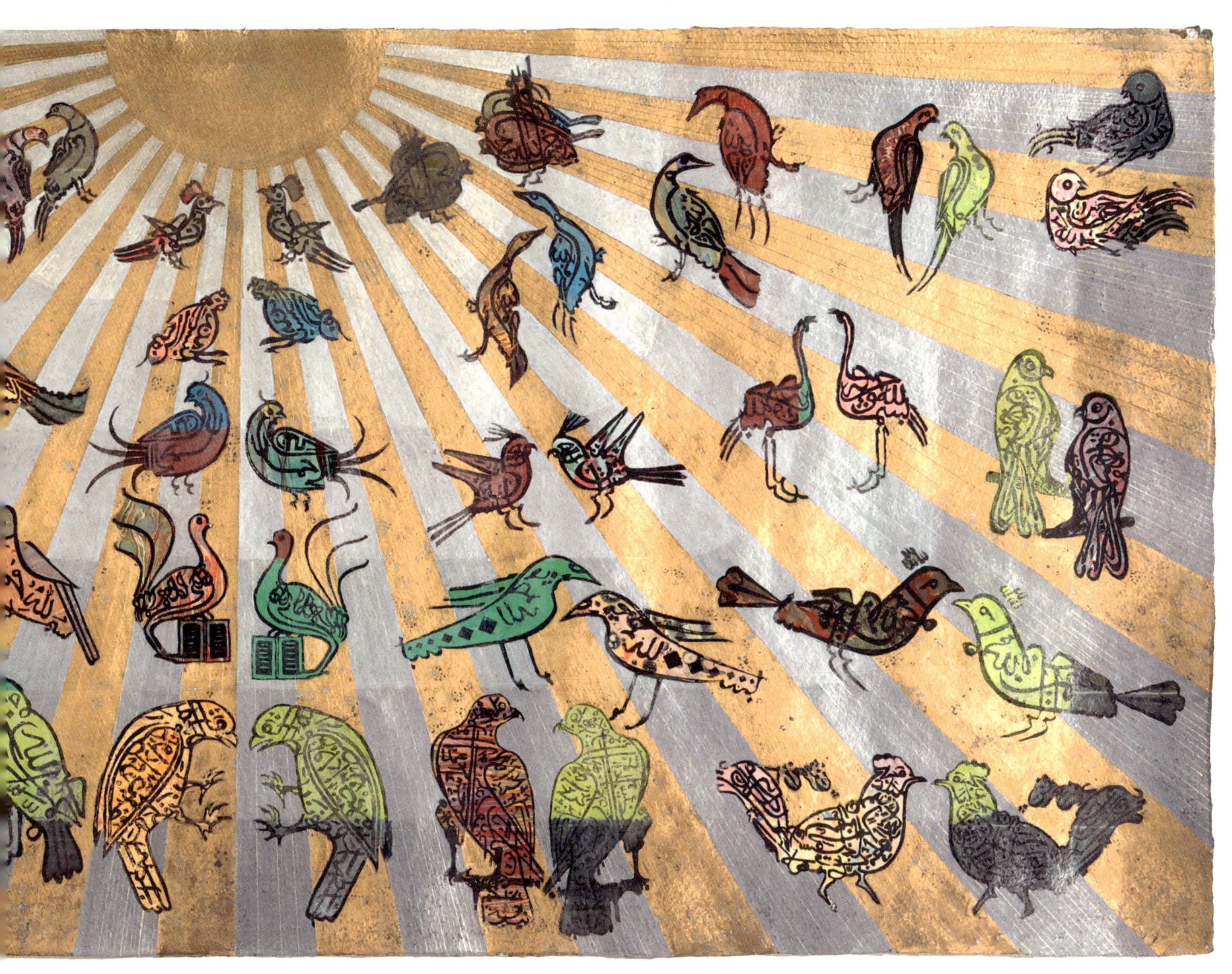

Monoprint and water-based paint on handmade paper, 80 x 170 cm, 2013. Private collection, Dubai

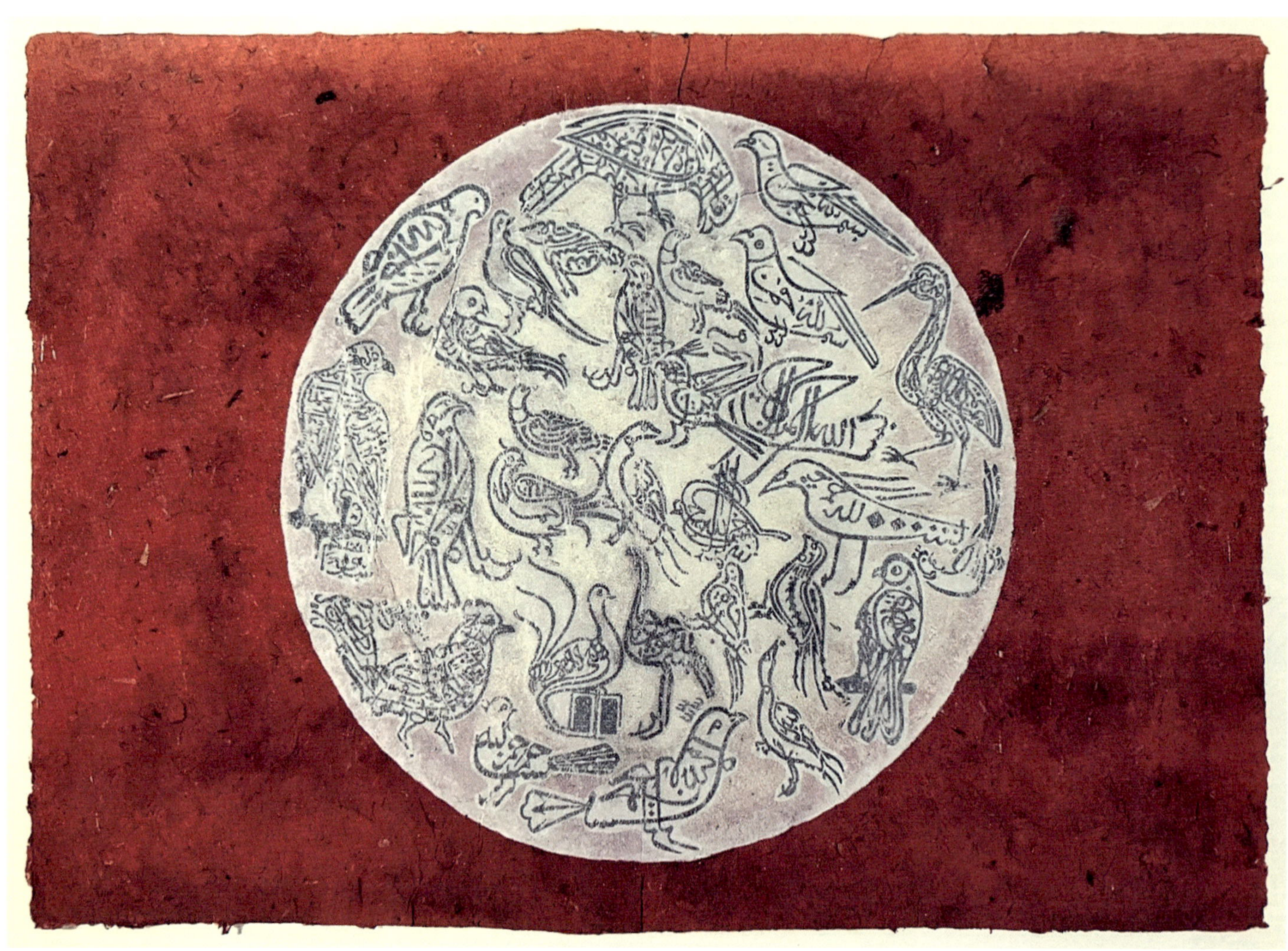

44   Monoprint and fluorescent paint on handmade Indian paper, 83 x 106 cm, 2001. Collection Susan Derges, Devon, UK

But if you are a lover, blush with shame;
Sleep is unworthy of the lover's name!
He watches with the wind throughout the day;
He sees the moon rise up and fade away [...]

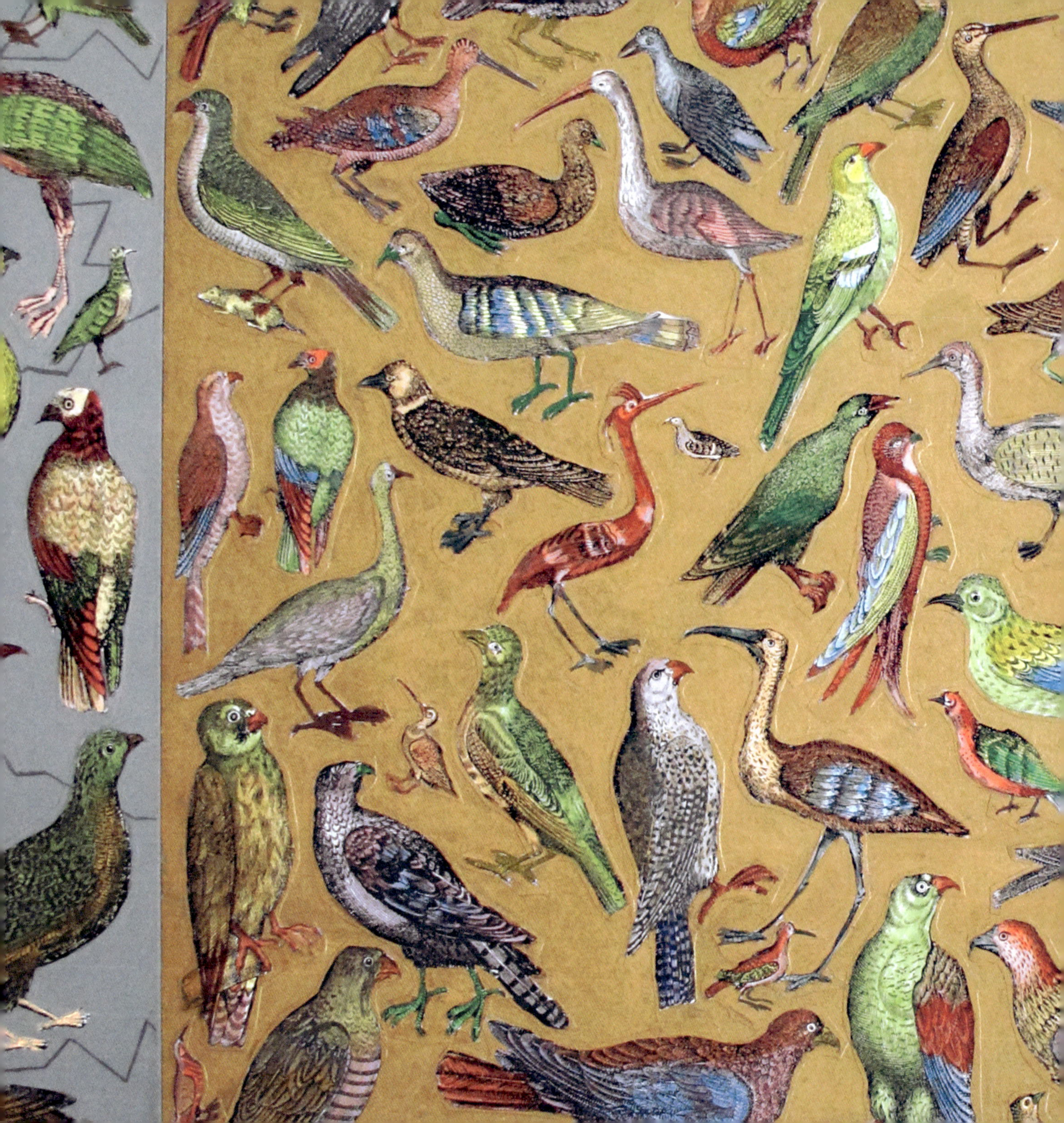